Praise for *Edna's Gift*

"Rudnick's debut memoir examines her complicated relationship with her developmentally disabled sibling as well as her own tumultuous path to self-acceptance and fulfillment. . . . Rudnick is a talented writer, often displaying a keen ability to capture emotional intensity through concise prose."

—*Kirkus Reviews*

"This astonishingly candid memoir explores a lifetime of memories, emotions, incidents, challenges and triumphs. We learn how the two sisters impacted each other through the decades of their unique relationship."

—Emily Perl Kingsley, parent, Emmy-winning writer,
author of "Welcome To Holland"

"Two lives that forever intertwine will draw you in and keep you reading. Each is slightly broken but uniquely whole . . . This book will stay with me for a long time."

—Kay Berry, an administrator of MRKH Experiences,
Advice and Support

"The relationship between 'typical' and 'special needs' siblings is complicated—often not reciprocal in the traditional sense and sometimes fraught with conflicting emotions, it can also bring unexpected riches. Susan Rudnick has given us an eloquently crafted exploration of how her life has been shaped by her sister. The result is an honest, insightful and love-filled memoir."

—Theresa Sullivan, author of *Mikey and Me*

"Beautifully written. . . I literally could not put it down."

—Barbara K Schwartz, PhD, author of *Hopeful Paths*

"A powerful and intimate account of the trials, tribulations, challenges, and opportunities of being a sibling of a person with disabilities."

—Avidan Milevsky, PhD, Ariel University,
author of *Sibling Issues in Therapy*

" . . . I love this book for its honest telling, for the transformational power of understanding that is the heart of the story, and for its beautiful clear prose."

—Susan Hadler, author of *The Beauty of What Remains*

Edna's Gift

Edna's Gift

How My Broken Sister Taught Me To Be Whole

Susan Rudnick

She Writes Press

Published 2019
Printed in the United States of America
ISBN: 978-1-63152-515-5
ISBN: 978-1-63152-516-2
Library of Congress Control Number: 2018956768

For information, address:
She Writes Press
1569 Solano Ave #546
Berkeley, CA 94707

She Writes Press is a division of SparkPoint Studio, LLC.

Names and identifying characteristics have been changed to protect the privacy of certain individuals.

In Memory of Edna

Remember the red wild flower
you found by the stream
last summer
vibrant
delicate
rare
and so hidden
from my eyes?

You are that rare flower
And the one who finds one.

And for all my MRKH sisters, everywhere

There's a blaze of light in every word
It doesn't matter which you heard
The holy or the broken hallelujah
~ Leonard Cohen

Prologue

On the day of the fire drill, it became clear that my sister, Edna, was different from other people. Different from me.

I was seven. Edna was six.

The bell had sounded three times and my second grade class at PS 90 in Richmond Hill, Queens, was ready. We stood at our desks waiting for Miss Kruger to tell us to get in line with our partners. She reminded us that there was to be no talking. We were to move quickly down the hall and outside, and then stand in line in the schoolyard until the fire drill was over. Before we went back inside, I looked for Edna, but I couldn't see her.

That's because while the rest of the school waited in the yard for the drill to be over, Edna sat alone in her first-grade classroom. She couldn't button her coat by herself or walk as fast as her classmates. Her teacher, Mrs. Dawkins, didn't want to spoil her speed record and risk not getting the class commendation, so she'd left Edna behind.

"What happened?" I asked Edna at the supper table.

"I waited," was all she said.

My sister Edna was both the most comforting and the most maddening person I've ever known. She was also my greatest teacher and I would have been lost without her. Growing up together, she was the officially challenged one—until as a teenager, I discovered my own invisible handicap. But it is only now, decades later, that I can see how our intertwined lives were spun from wholeness and unconditional acceptance, as well as deficit and disability.

PART 1

Chapter 1

Until we started school, Edna was my most treasured companion. We shared blue eyes and Buster Brown haircuts, and almost every night I crawled into her bed. With her soft skin, she was so cuddly, so squeezable. I felt safe when I was close to her.

On the small farm where we spent summers, we collected oval white stones from the beach so we could put them in the henhouse to fool the chickens and the farmer who came to gather the eggs. And once she stood with me all morning in the hot sun, waiting for customers to come to my lemonade stand, even though nobody showed up, and I told her she didn't have to stay.

Our tight bond provided a refuge from the acrimony between our parents, Eva and Ernest. Their relationship was the mismatch of displaced Holocaust refugees. They had married after having been separated and living on different continents for five years. When they arrived in New York in 1944, my mother was pregnant with me. Edna was born one year later. While our parents struggled to find their footing, Edna and I clung to each other.

I couldn't know then how, from that time on, I would carry Edna's sweet essence inside me like a precious gem wrapped in velvet. Yet, as each year brought with it new physical and mental challenges that I could master but she couldn't, the gap between us widened. But during that summer on the farm when I was turning six and Edna was almost five, we were just kids, inseparable, brimming with joyful plans and adventures.

One morning right after breakfast, we rushed to open the screen door. Our bare feet loved the warmth of the stone path under the trellis of sky-blue morning glories and the coolness of the grassy yard beyond, still damp with dew. In the corner of the yard, I reached for the tire swing. Holding it steady, I helped Edna climb into the bottom. Then, grabbing the rope, I scrambled on top and started swinging as fast as I could. Suddenly, I was high up, touching branches, peering through leaves. Edna couldn't make the swing go the way I could when I was five, but that's just how she was. I held the rope tight and pushed with my feet, and pretty soon we were both flying. She was scared and gripped the edges, but I was good at this, and she trusted me. When I jumped off, I tipped the tire so she could climb out.

Unlatching the gate, we dashed into the big daisy-filled meadow to see Toots, the brown-and-white cow. We loved Toots, especially because we had learned how to milk her. One at a time, we'd sit on a stool as Floyd, the farmer, put our hands on the warm, wrinkly udders and told us to squeeze and pull down until some drops of milk fell into the pail. When a fly buzzed around, Toots stamped her foot, and a wrinkle spread across her whole stomach. As we wandered through the tall meadow in our new matching shorts and halter tops, we pushed the grasses aside to clear a path. Sometimes we stopped to pull up long stems to suck and chew on. We didn't have to talk because we knew what we were searching for. We kept at it, using both our hands and our feet to push the grass to one side so we could see the earth. Every so often we came upon a rock to stand on, which gave us a better view of the field.

"I think I found a good one," I called out. "Come over here. We can both fit on it."

"I'm coming," Edna answered. With her arms helter-skelter and toes splayed, she ran toward me.

First I tapped it gently with my big toe. The top was dry and crusty and warm from the sun. Very promising. Next, I placed my whole foot on the sunbaked surface, still just skimming it, toes curling and uncurling, feeling the warmth and dry scratchiness.

"Should I step in it?" I asked her.

"Yes," Edna urged gleefully.

"You won't tell this time?"

"I won't," she promised, and I knew she wouldn't.

First one foot and then the other, pressing hard. And there it was, cracking, like cool, brown, chocolate pudding oozing between my toes.

"C'mon, you too," I said. "Step in it."

I held her hand, and then we were both in it, mushing the soft, squishy, glorious, goopy stuff between our toes. Just the two of us, together, in Toots's cow pie.

Maybe because we kept running through the grass afterwards, my mother never even noticed. Our secret always.

That was the summer of 1950, before I started first grade and Edna started kindergarten. That was the summer before everything changed, forever.

Chapter 2

I STOOD IN FRONT of the librarian's large wooden desk in the children's section, having already pushed last week's stack of books through the return slot. In first grade, I could already read chapter books.

"Do you have any books about handicapped children?" I asked, in my most serious, grown-up voice.

Edna and I were in our room playing when I overheard my mother refer to her that way. *Handicapped.* Our mother was on the phone with her friend Rosi. By then, I was aware that Edna was having some kind of trouble in school, but I didn't know any details, and my parents didn't offer any. Even now, I don't know if they kept their worries to themselves to try to protect me, or whether they were simply too overwhelmed with the grim information that was trickling into their lives to consider how it might affect me. In any case, I never thought of asking them to help me understand what was happening. It seemed up to me to figure this out.

The gray-haired lady with glasses on a chain around her neck and a pencil behind her ear looked up and stared at me.

"Let me see what I can find. We don't get too many requests like that," she said, putting her glasses on. She walked over to the wooden card catalog at the other end of the room and bent down over a low drawer. I followed her but stood back, watching her flip through index cards. Finally, she took the pencil out from behind her ear, wrote something down on a pad of paper and walked over to a shelf under a window. I watched as she ran a long fingernail across some books and then lifted a hardcover from the shelf.

"I found this one," she said, putting it in my hands. "Maybe this will be good."

She turned around and walked back to her desk. I closed my eyes, feeling the smoothness of the plastic cover. The book was about the size of my school notebook. I ran my fingers along the edges of the pages. It was a thin book. And then I opened my eyes. On the cover was a boy dressed in a robe with a hood and a belt around his waist, and he was leaning on crutches. He looked poor and raggedy, like someone from the distant past, maybe the Middle Ages. This boy didn't look anything like my sister. He looked like people who couldn't see or hear or walk, people who were crippled. People who had something wrong with them.

Edna didn't look anything like that. She didn't look different from other people. Yet, Edna was different. I was taking piano lessons and Edna wasn't. Her fingers couldn't play the keys right. And I had a best friend, and Edna didn't have any friends.

Still, there was something about Edna and the boy on the cover that was the same, even though they were different. Even though he was from a long time ago, the boy had something wrong with him, and Edna had something wrong with her. When you first saw her, you couldn't tell, but when she started to walk, you could tell. When she was singing, you couldn't tell. When she smiled, you couldn't tell. When I tickled her, I couldn't tell. But the other kids knew. And the librarian knew.

Edna was handicapped. And handicapped meant there was something wrong. She was crippled. It was just in a different way.

And now I knew.

Chapter 3

REMEMBERING THAT BOOK in my hand is to travel back in time. That was the first of a lifetime's worth of attempts to master the pain of our difference. As soon as I tried to understand what made Edna different, I encountered people who shunned her and professionals who labeled her as *developmentally disabled* or *retarded*. I learned to feel ashamed of her, and ashamed of my shame.

I became devoted to fixing what was wrong. If I could help my sister, maybe she would be okay in the eyes of others. And then we would both be okay. As deeply as I loved and appreciated her just the way she was, I grappled with how she was perceived by the outside world, and what that said about me. I was carrying two conflicting realities. Back then this was just something I did. I was unaware of the precious lessons I was learning: that there can be different, even opposite, ways to perceive a situation; that there is no one truth; and that it is important to listen for and trust the truth that lives in the depths of one's being.

But as an eight-year-old, I was lucky enough to encounter someone who did reach down into my depths. And that's when I discovered my life's calling.

Ever since Edna started first grade, the bedroom I shared with her was off limits after school. Either Estelle, the tutor, or Jo, the occupational therapist, was in there helping her. As early as kindergarten, it became apparent that Edna wasn't keeping up. My parents hoped that with enough support, she could catch up and stay in the regular classes. I hoped so too as I stood in front of the closed door, listening to a drum and Edna singing. I had no idea how these people were helping her, but it was clear how important it was to my mother for Edna to learn to do all the things she couldn't yet do. She couldn't skip or jump rope or hold a pencil between her fingers or play jacks. And when she walked up stairs, she couldn't put one foot over the other. She would clutch the banister, put one foot on a stair, and then slowly bring the other one next to it. I would have to wait while she stood in place for a long time before starting again. There were many times when I tried to teach her to "walk over." I'd stand next to her and wrap my fingers around her ankle, and then try to lift her foot from the lower stair to the one above.

"It's a little bit hard," she would say. But she was always willing to try again.

Still, the next time it wouldn't work either, and, frustrated, I would run up the stairs to the landing and bounce my ball really hard against the wall. Why couldn't she learn how to walk up a flight of stairs? What was so hard about that?

My father didn't seem to understand either. I could tell, because sometimes when Edna cried, he would get mad and yell in German, and my mother would say, "Ernest, don't be so impatient." At other times it was my father who would say, "Eva, stop pushing her so hard." When they argued, I would bury myself in *Mary Poppins*, my favorite book. I loved the part where they all went to the zoo at night, only to find it was the people who were in cages.

Yet, Edna could sing really well, and she had learned to read. Even when she held the book upside down, she could understand the letters. And no matter what else was going on, I could still climb into her bed at night and hug her. For me, she was not only cuddly and pretty with her rosy cheeks, but so loving, so reliable. We would talk and sing until one of us would say, "I'm not saying any more words, and that is period."

One day when Edna was seven, my mother took her on the subway to Manhattan to be tested by a psychologist named Dr. Michael-Smith. With all the help she was getting, Edna wasn't learning fast enough.

"It was fun," she told me afterward. "He has a poodle.

My mother added, "The doctor thought it would be a good idea for you to get tested too, so I've made an appointment for you.

"Why?" I asked.

"He wants to get an idea of how you're doing. It won't be like a school test. He'll just talk with you and play some games."

"What did he say about Edna?"

"That there are some things she is very good at that we didn't know about."

"Like what?"

"She has a very good memory, and she can remember things that other children can't. But," she hesitated, "it can be harder for her to answer questions like, what does the American flag stand for? That is called abstract thinking."

I was beginning to understand a little better. Edna had the kind of mind that could do one thing but not another. She could read books and say all the names of the characters, but she couldn't say what the book was about. What would the doctor say about me? He didn't have to tell me I was smart, because I got "outstanding" in everything on my report card. That I wasn't so good in art? That I played the piano? I already knew that. I couldn't wait to find out what else there might be.

Maybe there was something really special, something I was so good at that I knew nothing about.

My mother and I got out of the elevator and walked down a long hallway with plaid carpeting. Next to the buzzer, I saw the sign: H. Michael-Smith, PhD.

"What does the H stand for?" I asked.

"Harold," my mother answered.

"I thought his first name was Michael."

"Michael-Smith is his whole last name, and the PhD means he's a doctor."

"Harold Michael-Smith," I repeated to myself. I didn't know a first name could be a last name.

I rang the buzzer, and a door opened into a waiting room with a dollhouse in one corner and a basket of books in another. There was no poodle.

A short man with red curly hair and freckles walked toward me, smiling and reaching out his hand. He didn't look official at all, nothing like I'd imagined. As I took his hand, I noticed that it, too, was covered with freckles.

"Sorry, Peter the poodle isn't here; he's having a haircut. He would have liked to meet you."

He motioned for me to follow him into his office and closed the door, leaving my mother behind in the waiting room. He slid a chair out from a smooth wooden table for me and then invited me to get comfortable. Seated across from me, he took out a stack of cards.

I was sitting very tall, trying to be very grown up. I couldn't wait to find out what this testing business was about.

"Ready?" he asked. "I'm going to show you some pictures that have all kinds of designs on them, and I want you to tell me what you see."

I looked down at a white, shiny card with a lot of black curlicues, blotches, and wavy lines. I closed my eyes and thought hard. "Two flamingos in a puddle," I said proudly, opening my eyes.

"Good, and what are they doing?"

"They're playing."

The next one had some red in it. "It's a dragon, but not a very scary one."

It was a game of imagination, really fun. After no time at all, he was shaking my hand again, telling me how much he enjoyed meeting me, and I was back in the waiting room.

A week later my mother came into my room and said, "Dr. Michael-Smith wanted me to tell you how well he thinks you're doing, and that seeing you gave him a good idea. He thinks Daddy and I could use some help and he recommended a therapist for each of us."

All of a sudden I felt so light. I was like a kite, lifting higher and higher until I was floating way above the cars and the stores, our apartment building and even the trees. Dr. Michael-Smith had understood that I was okay, but that my parents needed help. And that was the truth. Someone who didn't know me knew me. Someone who didn't know our family saw me. Someone dove into the middle of our family, scooped me up into his arms and I was no longer alone.

How did he know how burdened I felt? And what did it have to do with pictures of butterflies and crabs? How was that possible? Did he know how my parents fought all the time? I hadn't told him that. I hadn't told him that Edna didn't have friends or that the teacher had left her in the classroom during the fire drill.

My father would often tell my mother, "You are being unrealistic."

And my mother would stalk out of the room looking angry, her lips pursed. She just wanted Edna to get on a normal track.

Dr. Michael-Smith had understood exactly how it was for me in this family. How I tried to help, but couldn't fix Edna or my parents. He had spoken magic words. This is what the letters PhD meant.

When you were a psychologist, you somehow knew what the truth was, without a person having to say it.

At eight, I had experienced the gift that deep listening can bring to a painful situation. I was on fire. I decided then that I was going to learn how to do what Dr. Michael-Smith did. One day I would be in my office, and when the buzzer rang, I would shake hands with a little girl and then invite her to come right in and make herself comfortable.

Chapter 4

THE PART OF me that wanted to learn everything I could to help Edna inspired me to become curious about why people were the way they were. It was how I wanted to see myself: as a budding altruist and intellectual. Yet, my longing to have friends and fit in could throw me into gut-wrenching conflict; sometimes I didn't want to care so much.

While I was in the top group in third grade, Edna had been left back in first. That was a huge blow to me. It was the first official marker of our differences. I was moving forward and she was already falling far behind. It felt overwhelming and scary. My mother explained that Edna would continue to have Miss Kruger as a teacher, and that felt comforting. Miss Kruger cared about Edna. This was at least a plan, and my mother was in charge.

Still, I was left with the issue of having recess on the playground at the same time as Edna. It was hard enough trying to get the girls in my class to like me without worrying about my sister, who had no friends at all. On one particular day, I felt more torn apart than ever before.

I was sitting in the lunchroom with Kitty and Linda, two of the popular girls in my class. Kitty was unwrapping her sandwich, taking her time unrolling and folding back the aluminum foil into neat squares. I could see it was tuna on white with the crusts cut off.

"This is too dry," she said, shaking her dirty-blond ringlets and putting it down.

"Looks good to me," I wanted to say, but didn't.

Linda, with her dark, straight ponytail, took even longer opening her lunch box, then rummaged around in it and fished out an apple.

"That boy Bruce is so stupid," she said, waving the apple in front of her, but not taking any bites.

Even though I was really hungry, I opened my lunch box slowly, doing my best to imitate Kitty. I began to unwrap the sandwich that I had made the night before. As I did, Kitty wrinkled her nose.

"Oh, no," I groaned. "My mom did it again, liverwurst and pickle on rye!"

"Liverwurst and pickle?" they both exclaimed.

"Well, sweet pickle," I said, my voice trailing. "You know it's that German thing. It's where my parents came from."

They turned toward each other. I was losing ground fast.

"You know Bruce, the way he holds his pencil," Linda went on, as both girls began to giggle.

I sat there watching them not eating their sandwiches and not understanding what was so funny about the way Bruce held his pencil. I watched as Kitty finally took a bite from the center of half her sandwich, and then put it down. Next, she lifted the other half, took one bite and put that down. I knew I was going to have to eat my sandwich really slowly, with the right pauses between bites, so I could end up finishing when they did. I watched Linda crumple her whole sandwich into a ball and stuff it back in her lunch box.

"Why did you do that? I'll eat it," I wanted to say, noticing the pickle juice from my sandwich landing on my skirt.

It was early April and warm enough for us to play outside after lunch. Walking across the schoolyard, I made my way past the girls who were playing Double Dutch jump rope, a game that involved swinging and jumping across two ropes, which I had yet to master.

As I passed a group with Kitty at the center, she called out to me, "We need a rope turner."

Wow, I thought, maybe they like me. I sucked in my breath and tried to look nonchalant as she handed me one end of a long rope. She picked up the other end and we started swinging it in an even, slow rhythm. I was loving the *thunk* sound it made as it hit the yard over and over. My stomach sent up little rockets of excitement. I had been chosen to be in the game with the popular girls!

One at a time, girls waited their turn to do two jumps while the rest chanted the alphabet, two letters at a time. After each girl jumped, she had to duck her head and not get caught in the rope so she could run around to the other side. When the rope snagged someone, the alphabet started over.

With one hand turning, I nudged my jacket off with the other and threw it on the ground so my arms could move more freely. AB, the first person jumped, and I looked away from the game for a moment.

And there she was in a corner of the yard, talking to herself, her hands gesticulating in front of her mouth in some kind of wild language all her own. It was a mistake to look. I turned back to the game: CD, EF. I couldn't help it; something in me made me turn my head again. I saw her stop and stand there quietly for a second. And even though her new navy blue spring coat had the buttons in the wrong holes and was askew on her shoulders, she mostly looked like other kids. Just a girl standing there with long slim legs, short brown hair in a bowl cut, and dark blue eyes. But when she started moving it was all over. I turned back to the game. GH, IJ, KL, I was back in the sway of it. MN, and I spun around again to watch her.

Now she was in the corner of the yard, circling in a jerky way, her head bent down, caught up in her own little world. Why did she have to be there? Why did I have to see her?

Then I felt the thickness of the rope, tight in my hand, bringing me back to the game. I felt the pull of it between Kitty and me as we swung it up in the air, and it arced over and circled down. This was so important. I belonged here, with the popular girls.

ST, UV, my stomach contracted and my neck started to turn, and there she was again. She was so there, in the corner of the yard. Now my legs started to feel stiff as sticks, and I was just going through the motions of turning the rope, while my thoughts kept piling up. Who was she talking to? What was she saying? Does she know the other kids think she's weird? How many of the other kids know she's my sister?

Then I remembered. I was supposed to play with Edna today. This was my day. I promised Mommy I would play with her in the school yard one day a week so she wouldn't have to be all alone. My mother had told me I was a good girl, and she knew it wasn't so easy for me, so she was going to pay me ten cents each time I did this. For ten cents I could buy ten strips of candy buttons on paper, or five sticks of chocolate licorice. Or I could add it to my fifty-cent allowance to get French fries that the fish store sold on Fridays. They were greasy, in little wax paper bags, and they were the best in the world. Now I felt tight inside, having taken the money, knowing that I wasn't going to play with Edna today.

Kitty didn't have to think about any of this, but I did. I wished Edna would just disappear. I wished I would disappear. I could never tell anyone about these terrible thoughts, not even my best friend, Janet, who cared about Edna.

I promised myself I would play with my sister tomorrow. Tomorrow would definitely be the day.

Today, I just wanted to jump rope.

Let me be clear. Edna never asked me to play with her. That never would have occurred to her. I don't know what she felt or wanted, because expressing feelings wasn't in her nature. Yet, I'm pretty sure she wouldn't have faulted me for wanting to jump rope with the other girls. Nor did she, as she grew older, think of herself as having something wrong with her. She referred to herself as handicapped, but that was a fact, not a judgment. Oh, she knew there were things she couldn't do. She understood that she was "differently abled" about sixty years before the term was invented. Still, my eight-year-old self couldn't possibly know that Edna's way of being just who she was, without judging herself, would become a model for me as I grew up and struggled to find my own sense of self-acceptance.

Chapter 5

THOUGH THE DOCTORS had no explanation for Edna's difficulties, my mother did. I can't remember when she told me the story, just that I was quite young. My mother claimed that in 1945 when she was in the hospital ready to give birth, there was still a shortage of doctors because of the war. Instead of getting the doctor to deliver my sister when the time was right, the nurse did something to push Edna back in or keep her from coming out. The story felt ugly then and still makes me cringe. I have no way of knowing whether it was true. More importantly, this story was my first encounter with the possibility that the universe could let such a thing happen, that there was randomness, scarcity, and such a lack of proper care for my mother that it changed the course of Edna's whole life. How could it be that, because of this, she wasn't able to sit up straight until she was a year old? That she never learned to crawl? And when she finally walked, she couldn't do half the things I could do?

The older Edna was, the more frustrating it was for my parents to get an accurate diagnosis. The possibilities ranged from "she's just a bit delayed" to cerebral palsy to, finally, brain injury and mental retardation. This last was just a catchall for an assortment of physical and mental deficits that were not fully understood. And there was no acknowledgement of what Edna *could* do, like read or be sensitive to other people's feelings. Services and programs were pitiably few, but my parents never stopped searching for opportunities for my sister to learn and grow. I lived in a family that assumed we were alone on a raft in a big sea, but you had to keep scanning for the possibility of another boat. And sometimes one did show up.

When Edna was eleven, my parents discovered The Club, a recreational program in Manhattan for handicapped children. Maybe here, they hoped, she would find friends besides the school bus driver and Alice, who came to clean our apartment. For my part, I was relieved that every Saturday Edna had a place to go, allowing me to feel less guilty about spending time with the new friends I was making in junior high school.

On one of those Saturday mornings, I went with her. I had given in to my parents, who argued that it would be good for me to share Edna's life, as well as enrich my education, by being a helper at The Club.

I wasn't thrilled about going. Being in the advanced seventh grade class was using up all my energy; that was enough education for me. I was getting used to having new teachers for every class, taking French, algebra, and even reading Shakespeare in the original. To console myself, I put on the cool outfit I'd worn the first day of school: blue shirtwaist dress, buck lace-up shoes, and a dark leather shoulder bag.

Dressed up in her new plaid dress, Edna kept running to the window to see if the van was there.

"It's not for another hour, stop asking," I said, hoping it would never come.

"I can if I want to," she replied.

I turned back to my French homework, wishing I'd picked Spanish instead, because that choice determined the group I was in for all of my classes. I didn't yet know much about boys, but they seemed to prefer Spanish to French. Boys were a scary country I had never been to, and I was pretty sure that wearing glasses and braces and being chubby would not help me get close to them. I dreamed of dancing like Justine on American Bandstand, but I was competing with girls like Wendy and Ellen, who wore new sweater sets every day and lived in big houses in Jamaica Estates. They were the rarefied few in the top group. I fell into the nondescript large middle, and avoided the four total losers like a bad virus. I called that group The Brooms, because they were left to sweep up the crumbs.

After Edna convinced me to go outside, we waited on the sidewalk. Eventually, a large, tan-colored van pulled up, and I noticed a folded-up wheelchair in the back. A girl with blond, wavy hair who looked thin and delicate waved from the window. The driver got out and slid open the door.

"George, this is my sister, Susie," Edna proudly told him.

"Welcome aboard!" he said with a smile. "Meet Bonnie, this is her first time."

I forced half a smile and nodded in her direction.

Edna climbed in first and sat next to Bonnie, whose feet—and teeth—were in braces. I followed, relieved that I could sit next to Edna.

"Now we're going to pick up Fritzi," Edna said, "right?"

"Right you are," answered George. "We're off."

I had heard all about Fritzi, Edna's special friend. How they were both in the music group and how they both loved Rodgers and Hammerstein. We pulled up in front of a six-story, faded brick apartment building. Outside, an old man stood behind a wheelchair with a figure in it that was slumped over. Once again, George slid open the door.

"How are you this sunny afternoon?" Edna asked so cheerfully.

The figure in the wheelchair raised her head, and I took a breath in and held it.

Fritzi's head was much too large for the rest of her body. Thick glasses covered her eyes, and her mouth sagged. I wanted to keep staring because she looked so strange, but at the same time, I couldn't bear to look. This was Edna's special friend? Together, George and Fritzi's father lifted her out of the chair and into the van.

Her father leaned in. "Have a good time. Here's your pocketbook," he said, placing a small black patent leather bag in her lap, as if she were just a normal child going to a birthday party.

Now I was in the back and Edna sat between Fritzi and Bonnie.

Fritzi started to speak. I couldn't decipher a word, but Edna understood her perfectly. Something about a song. They started humming together. Why would she pick someone who looked like Fritzi to be her friend? Why couldn't she find a girl who looked more normal? Did it have to be someone so handicapped, almost the worst-looking person I could imagine? Edna wasn't anything like that. She wasn't nearly that handicapped. I didn't want to think about her being friends with this person. I scrunched up in the corner of my seat and stared out the window, watching rows of attached brick houses yield to industrial buildings. When I smelled the bread from the Silvercup Bakery in Long Island City, I felt relieved because I knew we would be going over the bridge into the city, and this ride would soon be over.

Then there we were, parking in front of a tall, gray stone building with a jumble of vans, makeshift ramps, and kids in wheelchairs and on crutches spilling out all over the sidewalk. Edna climbed out, and I followed her. Some of the kids were teenagers clustered in a group, laughing; some were little kids struggling to speak, strange sounds coming out of their mouths; some looked mostly okay. All these misshapen people, and they seemed to be having a good time. How was that possible? It was as if I thought, how could they dare to think that life still could be fun? Something about that hurt me. It was big, this hurt. I didn't understand my feelings. It was overwhelming to witness this strange world that Edna was part of. Did she really have to go here? Is this where she belonged? Standing there, I suddenly felt very young, and it all seemed too much. There were too many things gone wrong in one place. I felt guilty having these thoughts. These kids were just trying to have a good time. What was wrong with that? I still didn't know. I wished I'd never come. I just had to get through this afternoon, and then I was never coming back. Just this afternoon and then it would be over. After that I felt a little better. I was twelve. I could do this.

A minute later a woman with brown hair mashed behind her ears flung open the door. I noticed her dark eyes darting back and forth, absorbing the whole scene. As if she were a magnet, the kids turned toward her.

"I love you, Sue," a little boy called out.

"Hey, tiger," she responded.

In the next moment Sue bolted out of the building, striding quickly, even though one foot dragged behind the other with a pronounced limp.

"Watch where you're going, mister," she bellowed to a driver who was backing up dangerously near a child. Then she turned and grabbed a wheelchair and, with one hand, began pushing it up the ramp toward the building. On the way up she stopped to pat another little girl on the head. "You look so pretty today."

She paused at a group of teenagers. "Let's get the show going. You guys are responsible for the community meeting. I'm counting on you."

"Got it," said a boy wearing a baseball cap, giving her a salute.

I sensed how this woman was both tender and a little gruff, and how she reached out to each child in a special way. She seemed to be everywhere, with kids crowding around her, as if she were the Pied Piper. And now because of her, the disarray had magically turned into an orderly procession filing into the building.

So this was the Sue that Edna kept talking about, the social worker who ran the club. I felt like I wanted to follow her, too. I was entranced. She was like a magnet attracting me, yet at the same time,

I couldn't move. I was scared. I had never met anyone who affected people like this.

Sue was strong and powerful, yet she was limping, and her foot was encased in a special large black shoe. My mother had told me she'd had polio as a child. That meant she was part like Edna and part like me. She was normal, yet she understood about being handicapped. She'd had polio, but now she was fine. She was in charge, making things happen, helping people, and everyone loved her. I wanted to be with her. I wanted to be just like her. I wanted to be her. She even had my name. I'd never liked the nickname Sue, but now I loved it. I was going to watch her and just by being near her, I was going to feel so much better. I was going to become strong and powerful by helping people.

Dr. Michael-Smith was a man who had inspired me. But Sue was the first woman I could identify with as a strong helper, who could get right into the fray. In my first years as a social worker, she was a model for me as I worked with severely disturbed people.

I followed Edna and walked up the ramp to go inside.

"This is my sister," Edna said, pulling me toward Sue, even though I could see she was busy talking to three other people.

"That's lovely of you to visit," she said, fixing her warm deep eyes on me.

"I'd like to help out," I offered, wanting to stand next to her forever.

"We could use help in the game room," she said, "just down the hall, thanks," and then she turned back to the others.

I walked into a room with a long table. Only one boy in a wheelchair was positioned at the end of it. Big blue eyes peered up at me from a thin face.

I made myself sit down next to him, then introduced myself and asked his name.

"Billy," he whispered.

"Would you like to play a game?" I asked, noticing that Billy was kind of cute, even though he was so skinny.

"Go Fish," he said, still whispering.

"That's a good game," I said.

I dealt out the cards, and then realized I had to put them in his hands because he couldn't pick them up off the table. Once he held the cards, he became animated. He knew how to get rid of cards by letting them fall on the table. I would pick up the one he needed and place it in his hand. Without saying anything, we had figured out how to play together. He won three times. I was doing fine with him. It was as if I was laughing inside, that's how good I felt.

By now there were seven or eight other kids in the room, and a young woman who seemed to be in charge came over to me.

"You're helping out, that's great," she said. "Could you just take Karin to the bathroom? It's right down the hall."

Karin's limbs were long and thin. She could barely stand, but she had braces and could walk with help. I can do this, I told myself.

"Thanks," Karin said, as she held onto my shoulder and I navigated her down the hall and into the bathroom.

Then as I opened the door into the stall, I saw that I was going to have to go in with her. And once we were in and I got her turned around, I realized she needed help pulling down her pants. I couldn't believe it, but there I was in the stall with her, fumbling to pull down her pants. Which, thank God, had an elastic waistband and no zipper. I held both of Karin's hands as she lowered herself down to the seat. We didn't look at each other. She could barely sit because her legs had trouble bending, but somehow she peed. I was trying my best, but I was starting to feel nauseated. Was I supposed wipe her? I made a quick decision. No. If anyone asks, I'll just say I forgot. I held out my hands, she grabbed them, and I managed to reverse the whole process, tugging her pants back up over her knees. She sat patiently waiting and, finally, I lifted her up off the toilet seat, and walked her back to the game room. Nobody asked me anything. The counselor just nodded a thanks.

I wandered into a hallway and tried not to cry, but I couldn't stop myself. Now I wasn't so sure about this helping business. This wasn't going to be easy. I had taken Karin to the toilet, but I didn't know if I could do it again. I kept seeing the elastic on her pants and those legs that could barely bend, and hearing the sound of her pee hitting the porcelain bowl. Physical, up close, too close. I hated it, and I hated myself for hating it. This would be nothing for Sue, but she was a grown-up. I guessed I had some time to learn.

"How was your afternoon?" my mother asked, after we had climbed out of the van.

"Fritzi and I sang a lot. It was great," Edna said right away.

"I definitely don't want to go every week," I said, staring at the sidewalk.

"Well, it's good that you went," was all my mother said.

What could I say? Edna had a friend, and that was the most important thing. I could never tell her what had happened to me. Compared to Edna's life, taking a handicapped girl to the bathroom was nothing.

A few weeks later at the supper table, my mother announced that Fritzi's parents had called The Club to get our number, because Fritzi kept talking about Edna. They had invited us to visit them, and we were going on Sunday afternoon for coffee and cake.

"Goody," Edna said. "I can bring my record of *Carousel*."

"But, Mom, I have homework," I protested, hoping that was a good reason not to go.

"You'll have to find a way to get it done," she said in a tone of voice that meant, you're going.

We pulled up in front of the brick building in Astoria and rang the downstairs bell.

Fritzi's mother stood waiting, the apartment door wide open.

"It's so wonderful that you could come. Fritzi has been waiting all day. Come in, come in," she said, arms extended, hugging Edna and reaching out to hug me as well. I sidled away from her and kept my coat buttoned.

"Yes, yes, please, come in. Yes, it's so wonderful," repeated her stoop-shouldered, white-haired husband.

"I'm Edna," my sister said proudly.

"Wonderful, how wonderful of you to come."

All those *wonderfuls*! I felt embarrassed by how excited Fritzi's parents were. Eyes downcast, I marched down a long narrow hallway jammed with old photographs. In the living room, furnished like ours with Danish teak furniture, a low coffee table was piled with cups, plates, Danish pastries, cookies, doughnuts, pies and a huge chocolate cake. Edna was already standing next to Fritzi in her wheelchair, trying to figure out how to unlock the wheels.

"Oh how nice of you," said Fritzi's mother, walking over to the wheelchair and bending over to unlock it. "But that's not necessary."

"I know how," Edna said in a determined voice.

"Are you sure? Oh, okay, I guess that would be all right. We're just not used to having anyone else take care of Fritzi," she said, glancing at my mother.

My mother nodded. "Edna's a big strong girl. She can do it."

As Edna wheeled Fritzi into the bedroom, my mother sat down on the couch and arched her eyebrows at me. Which meant, you need to go into the bedroom with them. I shook my head, sat down next to her, and reached for a Danish.

There was no way in hell I was going into that room. Edna was better than me. She didn't care what Fritzi looked like. But I felt as if I would faint if I had to go in there and pretend everything was fine. The parents were so eager to have company that they had enough cake for a bar mitzvah. And my parents were just as excited. I should be happy for them, but when I turned toward the cake and all the folded napkins, I felt like crying. It was just friends visiting friends. But it wasn't just friends visiting friends. It was people trying to be like other people, only they weren't. They were just pretending to be normal.

No, I was just going to sit on the couch and make it look like I was paying attention. I would nod my head and not say anything, and picture myself in my new flowered dress at the upcoming spring dance, my first one ever. Marvin, the cute boy with curly brown hair and freckles whom I had a crush on, would ask me to dance a slow dance, and as we danced, I would feel as if I were floating away. I was going to sit on that sofa in silence all afternoon, and eat that cheese Danish and maybe the cherry one.

Finally, we were in the car going home, my parents chattering on and on about how gracious Fritzi's parents were, how much they had in common. Edna was humming to herself. I kept trying to block the image of Fritzi in her wheelchair. Then I thought, it's a good thing Edna had this day, because next week I'll be going to the dance, so at least she's had something special, too. Once again, I was trying to balance things out so I wouldn't feel so guilty. But it wasn't working. A dance was a big deal. It was about boys and dates and future boyfriends. Would Edna ever have one? I felt myself shrink, a cinch belt of fear tightening my insides. Grabbing Edna's hand, I closed my eyes. Even though the pain I felt was about having her as my sister, holding her hand and listening to her hum made me start to relax.

It would always be like that. I could feel such grief and distress over her limitations, yet at the same time, she was the person who, more than anyone, comforted me. Even as I wanted to push her away, she soothed me.

❀

The night of the dance, my parents applauded when I came out of the bedroom wearing my new outfit. I had on white pumps, a sleeveless dress with aqua and purple bands around the waist, and a swirling skirt dotted with aqua and purple flowers. My school was right around the corner, so I walked slowly, pretending to smell flowers along the way, trying to make sure I didn't get there before my friends. Standing in the doorway, I could see girls leaning against one wall and boys leaning against the other. Nobody was dancing. The gym looked cavernous. I inched my way along the girls' wall until I spotted Debby and Naomi hunched over the table with plastic bowls of pretzels, chips, and pitchers of grape Kool-Aid. They were both wearing the same shirtwaist dresses they wore to school. Maybe I was too dressed up.

Boys began asking girls to dance. How long could I stand there, eating pretzels and drinking Kool Aid? Walking right past me, Marvin asked Wendy, then Ellen, then even Ruth from the middle group to dance. Then he danced a slow one with Wendy. I sat down with my now empty paper cup. During any one dance there were girls who weren't dancing, but everyone seemed to have danced at least some of them. On the other hand, no one seemed to notice that I hadn't danced at all, one small thing in my favor. I thought of Edna at home; her new ungraded class with other handicapped children never even had dances. How long could we keep using the excuse that I was older to explain why she couldn't do all the things I did? I wished she were with me. She wouldn't care if nobody danced with me. I was her wonderful sister, no matter what.

Then to my surprise I looked up and realized that Whitfield, a very smart boy in my class, was walking toward me.

"Would you like to dance?" he asked, extending his arm.

It was a slow dance. He held his arms three feet away as we did the box step, which I'd practiced in front of the mirror. Since his feet were twice as long as mine, I had to take two steps to his every one. We never looked at each other, though I hoped someone noticed that I was dancing. My first dance ever. Even as Whitfield jerked me around, I didn't care. I was floating.

When the song was over, he gave me a stiff little bow. And then I realized that I wasn't any particular girl to Whitfield. He was making the rounds and dancing one dance with every girl in the class, bowing to each of us when it was over. It meant nothing that he had danced with me. He was just being polite. After him not a single other boy came over to me. I was officially a wallflower.

"I'm sorry," my mother said, when I came home in tears. "I remember the same thing happened to me."

She was trying to be sympathetic, but saying that just made me feel hopeless. I was a doomed misfit, just like her and my whole family, and this was the worst evening of my life.

A couple of months later, things were looking up. Debby and Naomi had invited me to a sleepover. Sprawled across a bed at one in the morning, we decided that the dance was creepy, and the boys were immature. Though we weren't the popular girls, at least I belonged to a group.

Which oddly brought me back to thinking about The Club.

My mother wasn't pestering me to go, but I found myself longing to see Sue again. It would be wonderful just to be near her. The only real bad part of my day had been taking Karin to the bathroom. I was never going to do that again. If anyone asked me, I could just say I didn't know how to do it. Funny, how I actually wanted to go back to The Club. It made me special in a way that the girls in my class would never understand.

A month later I was in the game room using dominoes to build a house as a little girl watched. Although she was in a wheelchair and her arms didn't work well, she was very pretty, with her dark hair in a ponytail and long black eyelashes. Her body had a normal shape, and I could understand her speech. When I finished, I put a domino in her hand and guided it over the table and we knocked the house down together, laughing.

"Did you hear about Billy?"

My ears picked up the words of one of the two counselors who had just walked into the room.

"Shhh," the other one whispered, pointing a finger at the table and placing a finger over her mouth.

They walked to a corner of the room. I got up and followed them.

"Is Billy coming today?" I asked, trying to sound casual.

"Oh, um, well . . . Billy passed away earlier this week," one of the counselors replied. "But that's not something we want to upset the others with."

A few weeks earlier, I had been playing with him, and now I would never see him again. Billy. Gone. He had been fragile, but now he wasn't here. Nobody else I knew had died. And the person who told me had no idea that I had played with him. There was nobody here who knew anything about me and Billy and the game we'd figured out. From a distance, I heard myself thanking her for telling me.

My feet found their way back to the table. I picked up a domino and began rebuilding the house. In my mind I saw Billy's hands holding his cards, but now they were all sliding out onto the table. His hands couldn't even hold the cards. I wished I'd never played with him. I had been so proud of playing Go Fish with him then, but now, so what? It didn't matter. He was dead. But then, I thought, maybe I'd been the last person who played a game with him. Maybe that was good. I hadn't done anything wrong, had I? The room was starting to spin. I couldn't stand the panic I felt. Just stare at the dots on the domino until there was nothing but white dots on blackness. And then there would be no table, no little girl, no feelings, no room, just the frozenness of white dots on blackness.

It wasn't until I became a therapist and took a course on trauma that I understood that there was a name for my way of escaping overwhelming pain: a coping mechanism called dissociation. As a child, it was just something I did: staring at something until time stopped and life went on around me, but I was no longer there. I could will it to happen, and sometimes did so when I was bored, walking down the street, or in class. Dissociation became my characteristic way of moving through life. When I bounced checks in college, my parents called me a dreamer. In my twenties, my ability to space out jibed with smoking marijuana: turning on, tuning in, and dropping out. Not having been a victim of incest, rape, or physical abuse, it had never occurred to me that trying to be Edna's good sister was its own form of trauma. So was being the daughter of refugees who had fled their homes to escape the rise of Hitler.

Chapter 6

My life with Edna unfolded on the larger canvas of our parents, who had met and married amid the turmoil of fleeing Nazi Germany. They had lived in several countries before landing in America. I had been conceived in Brazil and born just six months after they arrived in New York.

There were huge problems between them. My mother never wore a wedding band; she didn't even own one. They rarely hugged, and I never saw them kiss. They slept in separate beds on opposite sides of the room. All through my childhood, I longed for them to be more loving, with the kind of marriage I saw on 1950s TV shows. If Hitler hadn't come to power, I doubt they would have ended up together. Still, determined to be good parents, they had pieced together a home life in a fourth-floor walk-up apartment.

Our huge, black upright piano was at the heart of our sweetest times as a family. A majestic presence in our living room, it was our esteemed ancestor that my grandparents had somehow managed to transport from Germany. It grounded us, and for me it was a magnet of joy, a source of respite from worrying about how the world was treating Edna or how my parents were treating each other.

One afternoon when I was about ten, I watched my mother dust the curlicues and dots of the ornate carvings that rose from the piano's legs up over the cover and along the sides. Then she carefully opened the lid and caressed the inner nooks of each worn-to-softness ivory key, pulling forward over each black one.

I followed her beautiful hands as she finished cleaning and sat down at the keyboard. With her eyes closed and her hands arched gracefully over the keys, a Bach fugue poured out of her. When she finished I sat down next to her. All four of our hands were poised above the keys for a duet as she counted, and when she nodded our fingers touched down on the smooth keys. I was instantly drawn into her faraway, long ago world, in which classical music was part of her daily life. In the rush of sound and rhythm, trying to keep up with her, my mind relaxed. The music swam through both of us, and we became the music.

I felt this especially when we played Bach in a minor key. It was as if my mother's passion, along with the complicated story of her life, in some mysterious way entered me. In D minor I felt her strength, her love for me, and how much she wanted to convey to me the preciousness of life, even though it might be full of mistakes and suffering. My father was not her true love. They had met in their hometown, Nuremberg, in the early thirties, just as Hitler emerged as chancellor. Their brief romance faltered and, at age twenty, she immigrated to Palestine. At twenty-five, he left for Brazil. Yet, when the war broke out in 1939, she chose to reunite with him in Brazil. She later had regrets, but in the turbulent chaos of war, she remained with him, switching continents a final time to come to America. Whenever she spoke of these things, they seemed like disconnected facts that made no sense. I was full of questions. When I asked her why she'd left Palestine, she would tell me how an Arab had proposed to her and she would have been his second wife. But she didn't tell me that she'd loved or missed my father. It was up to me to piece together the reality that there was nobody in her life in Palestine. Why did he want to be with her? From my father, I could glean that he had nobody in Brazil and had still been taken with my mother. It's quite possible that she herself, traumatized by the refugee experience, had no way to explain her actions. But when we played the piano together, all the questions receded, and I let myself fall into a well of dark mysterious beauty.

Most afternoons I prepared for my weekly lessons. Even though I complained about having to practice so much, secretly I loved feeling embraced by the piano's magnificent size and the softness of the keys, and learning a piece so well I could play it by heart.

Still, sometimes I hated my mother and her way of seeing things. There were days when I was practicing that she came in from the kitchen, dish towel over one arm and criticized. "It's important to play the rests. I'm not hearing them."

She was so smart, but she was too smart. Always one up on me. Couldn't she just wear makeup and get a permanent like American mothers, instead of her severe, short hair? She didn't play mahjong or cards. Instead, she read books and underlined them, and tended to look down on people who weren't bookish. We never had Coke in our refrigerator. I longed for a mother who would be more relaxed and informal. My friends' mothers seemed to embody that way of being, while mine was intense and tense. I didn't want to have to understand her, though I sensed there was something wise she had to teach me. But I often filed away what she said for when I was older.

Edna didn't have the coordination to play piano, but we could sing together. My mother bought the *Fireside Book of Folksongs* and learned all the American songs, from spirituals to "The Arkansas Traveler." Edna and I would turn the pages, loving the illustrations of people playing banjos alongside miners with their pickaxes, careful not to loosen more pages from the taped together spine. We stood on either side of our mother as she played. I favored the intense action of "Drill Ye Tarriers, Drill," while Edna loved "The Twelve Days of Christmas." She knew the all the verses.

"You forgot the sixth day," she said. She needed to go in order, and it upset her if we skipped a day. "It's in the song; you have to sing it, Susan."

"Fine," I answered, wanting to poke her.

But the next minute her voice was so sweet, I wanted to cuddle up next to her.

I loved when my mother reminded us to sing with feeling, because Edna and I would give each other the "there she goes again" look, a glorious moment of being just like normal sisters, united about our annoying mother. Suppressing giggles, we sang in our "feelingest" way. And because he insisted he couldn't carry a tune, my father was our audience. He applauded from the couch, making my usually somber mother smile and offer us chocolate.

My absolute favorite time was Hanukkah, the only Jewish holiday we observed. The piano played the starring role in the celebration. One year, on the last night, a soft white linen tablecloth was draped over the top and piled high with presents wrapped in blue and silver paper. My mother filled our sterling silver menorah with multicolored candles and gingerly set it on the closed keyboard. Pan roasted-potatoes and a chicken sent fragrant crackles from the oven. After waiting for what seemed like forever, Uncle Ernst and Aunt Hannah finally arrived and added their presents to the pile. Then my mother lit the central shamas candle, and we sang the prayers as, one by one, we each lit a candle. Then my father picked up the menorah and placed it in front of a window for the whole neighborhood to see. Next, my mother opened the piano, and her long fingers lingered over the keys. In that lingering was a moment of her softness. I breathed it in. Then she began to play *Ma'oz Tzur*, a song about the many times God saved the Jewish people. Edna and I stood next to each other in our navy blue taffeta party dresses. And we all sang, first in Hebrew and then in English, all of us, even my father.

Chapter 7

One month after I started high school, my mother put down her coffee cup at Saturday breakfast and told us we were moving out of our apartment and the neighborhood. And though I worried that such a move would turn my life upside down, it was nothing compared to a different kind of move that would take place a few months later and change the course of my life forever.

But the move she was talking about that Saturday morning was meant to be a happy one. My parents had suddenly been able to put a down payment on a Tudor style house in nearby Jamaica because the German government had sent us money. This restitution wouldn't make up for my parents having to flee their home, but it was supposed to help us improve our lives. My father would be able have a flower garden, we would no longer have to schlep the laundry cart up and down four flights of stairs to the Laundromat, and Edna and I would each have our own room.

"And now we are going to take a ride to see it," my mother announced.

When I asked her about school and seeing my best friend or having my piano lessons, she explained that I would go to the same school, but instead of walking I would take the El train. She added that she was sure I would like having my own room. My no-nonsense mother wasn't interested in hearing my concerns. Just like when it was pouring and I was reluctant to go outside, she would tell me I wouldn't melt. The message always seemed to imply that my worries were nothing compared to her suffering as a young woman growing up in Germany, and I should just get on with it. At the time I attributed her callous attitude to being German, and I vowed to be softer, like Americans.

We got into the car, drove down Metropolitan Avenue, past the building where my best friend, Janet, lived. We crossed Lefferts Boulevard, my favorite street because it had all our special stores: the butcher shop, where the butcher always leaned over the counter to give me a slice of ham or liverwurst; the bakery, where we bought a special German plum cake, made only in October; and the Homestead Hotel, where I once had lunch with my grandparents, the only time they ever took me out.

Now we were in new territory. I had never walked this far. We passed a used car lot that took up a whole block and a gas station, but there were no apartment buildings or sidewalks. Here and there I spotted a dilapidated wooden house, mixed in with a locksmith shop and a store that rented tuxedos. The area felt washed out and lonely.

But soon after, we turned a corner and drove up a steep hill with trees everywhere. Though there weren't any stores, there were sidewalks in front of neat lawns with flowering bushes, and paths leading to the houses. This street reminded me of the ones on *Leave it to Beaver* and *Father Knows Best*, my favorite TV shows. It occurred to me that if I were going to be living in a house like that, with porches and dining rooms and mail coming through slots in the front door, maybe my life would be more American. Maybe I would have friends over to hang out in our backyard, maybe even a boyfriend.

"Be very polite to the Amerikaners," my father said as we parked in front of a house set high up from the street. There was a wrought iron staircase leading up to an oval shaped door.

"The Americans?" I asked.

"No, *Amerikaner* is their name," he answered.

Even their name had American in it. How perfect, I thought.

As we walked up the steps I also thought: how amazing, we now own a staircase. And there, near the bottom of the front door, was the brass slot for mail.

A woman with a scarf tied around the curlers in her hair answered the door. My mother never used curlers. But if she did, she never would have answered the door wearing them. This is what real Americans did.

As I peered into the living room, a girl around my age was coming toward us. She was slim, with every hair in her smooth brunette pageboy in place. Her dungaree cuffs were creased and folded, instead of being rolled up like mine. And even though she was wearing a loose-fitting shirt over her pants, I could tell that her bra size was at least a B cup. She would definitely be in the popular group. The girl's mother suggested that she show me her room, and motioning for me to follow, the girl leaped up the stairs without putting her hand on the banister. She opened the door to a small room with pale green walls, and then flung herself onto a bed piled high with stuffed animals. As I stood in the doorway, I noticed a built-in chest in the corner. I didn't care about stuffed animals, but I loved the chest. It could be a seat with a cushion. I instantly imagined myself on the seat with two friends lounging on the bed. I wanted this room.

My mother poked her head into the room and told me to come look at the attic. I followed her up a narrow staircase into a long room with slanted ceilings. She explained to me that now that I was a teenager, she thought I would like to have this private space, a whole floor to myself.

"Plenty of room for all your stuff," she said, giving me a look that meant, I thought this all out, and this is the room I want you to have.

"I don't want the attic," I replied, without hesitation.

"Why not?" she asked, genuinely puzzled.

"I want the room that the other girl has."

"Why?"

"I just really like it," I said. She would never understand how I just had to be like this other girl.

"But it's small, and Edna needs the bigger room for her therapies."

"I don't care about size. You told us we could choose our colors. And I should also be able to pick the room. I want it to be light green."

"If that's what you want," she said finally, clearly disappointed.

I didn't understand why she thought the attic would have been good for me or why she was disappointed. I guessed she thought that if she were me, she would have chosen the attic. But I wasn't her. I wanted to be on the same floor as everybody else. And the smaller room felt cozier. But she would not have understood any of that, and there was no way for me to explain.

"So what do you think about moving to the new house?' my mother asked us in the car on the way home.

"I'm going to miss the Spotkes," Edna said

"What are you talking about?" I asked, irritated. That was just the kind of thing Edna would sometimes come out with. The Spotkes lived right underneath us, but we didn't have much to do with them. Mr. Spotke worked at night, and Mrs. Spotke was always yelling at Frankie and Johnny, the two pudgy boys. Peggy, who was my age, used to come up to play with me, but after she started Catholic school, we stopped being friends.

"Why on earth would you miss them?"

"We won't see them anymore," Edna said, with her infuriating logic.

"So what," I pressed. "What about your new room and the backyard and all?"

"That's nice," was all she said.

I would have given anything to know what was going on in her head and what she really was feeling. She would rarely tell us. Yet, I did understand something of what she meant about the Spotkes. We had always lived on top of them, and now we would be just us. Alone. Edna's condensed way of expressing how a house was different from an apartment made sense. And while I wouldn't miss the Spotkes, I was going to miss other things we had always done: walking up the block to Wonderland Toy Store, continuing on to the playground in Forest Park, and then climbing the big rock that was tucked away on a side street. And really, as much as I yearned for us to be like the TV families, I also knew there was something special about where I had come from. I'd lived in a community where I felt embraced and safe, with so many families like ours. People who looked out for one another and understood the difficulties of having been uprooted, leaving everything behind. I realized, without ever having to ask, what the numbers on my parents' friend Xander's arm meant. They were visible when he used to push my swing. Still, pushing my swing meant he had survived and was now the father of two boys who were our friends. I could feel that there was something strong and proud in me that came from being part of that community. I was going to take that with me when we left.

For weeks after we moved in, I ran up and down the stairs of our house, outside and inside. At the second floor landing, posing like a movie star with legs crossed in my bathrobe, I would brush my hair and gaze down at the new baby grand in the living room. Or I would sprawl on the new pink cushion my mother had made for the chest in my bedroom and read movie magazines. Sometimes I would even deign to go down the basement stairs to switch the clean wash into the dryer.

At night, though, I still crawled into Edna's bed to tickle her and then squeeze her. Her room faced the backyard, and I loved to lie in her bed, looking out at the red maple tree branches that almost touched the window as they waved in the breeze. Sometimes moonlight shimmered through the leaves, and I was back on the farm, holding tight to the tire swing rope, as I flew through leaves and sky.

"Do you remember the farm?" I asked her.

"Tillie called me peaches and cream," she said.

I could see Tillie, who owned the farm, cutting up peaches to put in our cereal bowls, and pinching Edna's cheeks. I would be turning fifteen soon and should have been in my own room, in my own bed. Still, I pulled the blanket around us.

Edna was still peaches and cream to me.

I was just getting settled and comfortable when everything changed again.

On a warm May evening, we were eating supper on our new cedar picnic table on the screened-in back porch. I had cut pansies that my father had planted, and arranged them in a vase on the table. My mother brought out cucumber salad, home fries, and knockwurst. My father was drinking a mug of dark beer. It felt like a holiday.

Then I noticed my mother with her serious look. "Daddy and I have important news for all of us."

My dad cupped his hands around the mug. I dipped sausage into mustard on my plate.

She told us they had found a new camp for Edna on Cape Cod. There would be picnics and trips to the beach. That didn't sound so special. Edna had been going to a camp for handicapped children run by The Club for several years.

"And Edna, if you like it, you can stay there for school."

"What do you mean, stay there for school?" I asked.

"Just what I just said. Edna will learn a lot of new things. We're very happy about that, and you should be too. Edna has not been getting what she needs in her ungraded class, still stuck in an elementary school. What makes this possible is that the state has agreed to pay."

"I want to go there," Edna said right away.

"Why?" I asked.

"It's a good idea," she replied in her usual terse way.

"How do you know?" I kept on.

"I just do," she insisted.

I looked at her face for a clue about what she was thinking, but her bland expression told me nothing. It was no use trying to badger her. She seemed to sense that this was right, even if she couldn't explain why.

"Does that mean she's going to a boarding school?" I asked my parents, having a vision of an endless room lined with beds, like in the storybook, *Madeleine*.

"It's a residential school, with teachers and counselors and all sorts of helpers," my mother said.

Though she went on to explain that Edna would have a roommate and make friends, and we would visit, this was not adding up. My mother made it sound so wonderful, as if all the ways in which my sister was different and didn't fit in would no longer be a problem. Even at The Club, where most of the kids were physically handicapped, Edna didn't quite fit in sometimes. How could my mother be so sure about this new place? Besides, Edna at fourteen seemed too young to be sent away. I slipped off into my frozen, disassociated space. The table had been cleared when I came out of it.

That was the only time we talked about Edna leaving home. My parents didn't seem concerned, and Edna didn't ask any questions. My mother got busy buying her new clothes, and Edna tried them all on, even though she didn't like having things pulled over her head.

This was such an enormous change. Did Edna know that? I wanted it to be good for her and good for my parents. They were determined that she get a good education, so she could grow up and take care of herself. That took precedence over everything.

But for me, Edna was leaving and I already felt empty. This was not a situation that would occur on *Father Knows Best*, where everything got resolved in one episode and nothing drastic ever happened.

We both went away to camp that summer, me to an artsy one in the Berkshires, Edna to the new special one. And then I came home, but she didn't.

At first that was fine. I was high from a summer of hanging out with new friends, and entranced by endless discussions of boys we would or wouldn't kiss. Most importantly, I had fallen in love with guitars, banjos, frets, finger picks, and creased, handwritten chord charts. I loved leaning up against trees, singing ballads and protest songs, spirituals and Calypso. How glorious to be part of a group singing our hearts out, teaching each other chords and verses. The first time I held a guitar, my right hand started strumming the G major chord, and "This Little Light of Mine" came pouring out. I had to have one.

In late August, my parents took me to Matt Umanov Guitars. I came home with my wondrous birthday present, a second hand Favilla classical nylon string guitar. I spent hours lost in the sound of my hands thrumming the strings, breathing in the Weavers and Joan Baez. Oh, it's here that she pauses between the third and fourth line, and here where the chord shifts from major to minor. Then, standing in front of the mirror, I would perform my version. I had found my instrument and my music.

But on Friday afternoon of the first week of school, lying on my bed wondering how I would ever get all my honors English homework done, I suddenly missed Edna. The feeling caught me by surprise because, in a way, it was a relief not to have to worry about her being in that awful school or feel guilty about all the things I could do that she couldn't. I didn't have to tamp down my excitement over getting into the water ballet group at school, so she wouldn't feel bad.

Still, I missed her. I brushed my hair one hundred strokes and walked into her room. Her new aqua bedspread was stretched taut over the mattress. A clown pillow with red hair and a smiling face was propped against the pillow she slept on. And the air in the room smelled funny, like furniture polish. There was a hollowness about it. I lay down on her bedspread and ran my hands across its unwrinkled surface. I stared out of her window and had a dim awareness of leaves starting to fall. I tried to see if I could follow the path of one leaf all the way down to the ground. Leaf after leaf, I watched them land on the lawn, on a bush, on the neighbor's lawn. Edna was in East Sandwich, Cape Cod, so she could learn arithmetic and writing. What was East Sandwich like? I tried picturing her in a building near a beach, but all I could see was a dark brick wall. I couldn't see Edna. I didn't know what her room looked like, or what it was like for her to be away from us.

"My teacher's name is Edith, and we went to a nature park," was all she said on the phone.

I missed her, though not in the way of wanting to tell her everything about my day, because there was so much she couldn't understand about high school. What I missed was something I couldn't quite name.

But then the truth began to dawn on me. Edna never cared what grades I got or how popular I was. She never judged me in any way.

I was her big sister, and she just loved me and looked up to me, no matter what.

When I got 68 on an algebra test, she just said, "It's so hard, poor Susie."

It didn't matter that she had no idea what algebra was. She knew a lot more than most people about how hard it was to try something and not be able to do it. I had never before realized how much I counted on her. She was the person I came home to. She was home. I grasped this in that moment of lying on her bed, which was still her bed, even though she didn't live here anymore.

My sister was gone.

Except for vacations, we would never live together again. And though our paths would diverge, her accepting heart would live on in me, a source of comfort and strength when all else failed.

Part 2

CHAPTER 8

LIFE WITHOUT EDNA freed me up. I could go to a friend's house after school to do homework without worrying about what she was doing. The one time a boy picked me up to go to a party, I didn't have to explain her awkwardness. Being sexy and popular was a long shot, but now at least I had a chance for a normal American life. Still, I struggled with feeling fat, and whether to reward myself with a glazed donut as I schlepped my heavy book bag home from school.

My junior year rumbled along until one spring afternoon a doctor threw me a curve ball. I discovered my own handicap, only unlike Edna's, mine was invisible. Devastating, it threw my life into chaos, as I tried to understand why this was happening to me. And yet, it also felt strangely full of import because of Edna.

We were physically apart, but closer together than ever because now we were both damaged goods. As with my sister, my particular syndrome was rare and not well known or easily explained. There seemed to be no way for me to escape the fate of being tied to her by my defect, and I became even more obsessed with wanting to be "normal."

Yet inside of me there was a deeper truth waiting to unfurl. I didn't have words for it. But in my grief for myself, I held Edna close and loved her more. She might not understand my secret in all its complexity, but she would share my suffering.

Like a labyrinth where the way in becomes the way out, her ability to accept herself would point me in a healing direction.

It all started in a very casual way.

I was fifteen and hadn't yet gotten my period. I don't recall being bothered or curious about it, nor do I remember discussing it with friends. In my nerdy honors class, all we talked about was our crush on our history teacher and our grades on the last test.

But during a recent visit to my pediatrician, Dr. Blumberg had palpated my stomach, and then taken a small flashlight to peer between my legs. He recommended a more thorough exam under sedation in the hospital, followed by a consultation with a specialist. He had been very matter of fact in suggesting this, and it had never occurred to me that I had anything to worry about.

On the day I met with the specialist, my mother stayed in the waiting room as an unsmiling nurse directed me down a long hallway and into a windowless room. I had undressed, inched up on a high table, put my feet in metal stirrups and covered myself with a sheet. I was freezing, and my vagina was exposed. A man in a starched white lab coat opened the door. He had a mustache and his face was all red.

"I'm going to take a look at you," he announced.

I could feel the heat of him as he leaned over me. For the first time I felt frightened. I shivered and began staring at a wrinkle in the wallpaper, spacing out till I had gone away.

From afar I could hear him saying, "You can get dressed now."

I got dressed as if I were someone else putting on my clothes, and found myself in front of a massive desk. The red-faced man sat behind it. My mother was next to me, but I couldn't feel her presence.

"What we have here is a serious situation. You need plastic surgery with skin grafts. It will take about two months to recover."

What was he talking about?

"What about my period?" I ventured.

"You will never menstruate. You were born with no uterus, no cervix, no vaginal canal. You can't menstruate like most women. You do have ovaries, but you will ovulate directly into the bloodstream. And you will need surgery to create a vagina out of the dimple that is there, so you can have intercourse."

The room got really big and the doctor receded. "No period, no uterus," reverberated in and out of my ears. Nothing to grasp, except that it would take two months of recovery.

"What about camp?" I said, sputtering out the words.

"You won't be able to go to camp if you have the surgery done this summer. That way, you won't have to miss school."

My head felt frozen onto my body and I couldn't even turn to look at my mother, who remained silent. The words, "no camp," kept echoing inside me. I had been so excited to have been accepted to a special teen camp to work with disadvantaged children.

My mother and I walked out of the office together. All of a sudden I remembered her grim face when we'd left the hospital after I'd been examined under sedation.

"You already knew this!" I screamed. "Why didn't you tell me?"

Her eyes were closing. "I wasn't sure of it then," she said. "I didn't know what to do. And I never thought the doctor would just blurt it out like that."

"How could you do this to me?"

I glared at her for a moment and then bolted away. Out the door, down the block. I briefly turned around to see her walking with her head down. I could think of nothing but needing to escape from her. Down the subway stairs, fumbling for a token, into the train, out at the right stop, up the hill to my house and into my room. Everything went dark.

About half an hour later my mother knocked on my door.

"*No!*" I yelled.

"I'm sorry this happened. But we have an appointment with another doctor for a second opinion. Let's wait and see what he says."

I lay on my bed in a fetal position facing the wall. I didn't want my mother anywhere near me. It was Edna I tried to picture, tucking me in and telling me I was fine. But even that wasn't working.

I don't remember when I told my sister about my troubles, but I can imagine the conversation. It would have taken place some years later, when she was living in a community among families with young children. I would have told her about how I could never get pregnant.

"That's sad, poor Susie," she would have said.

And when I shared my wish to adopt, her response might have been, "I like that idea. When will that be?"

"Well, first I need a husband."

"That's okay, you'll find one."

Fully aware that she could never have a child, Edna encouraged me anyway. She seemed to understand and accept how that would be beyond her capacity.

But that conversation took place years later, and after the doctor's pronouncement, I just felt bereft. I was glad that the following day I had an appointment with Elliot, the therapist I'd started seeing a month before. When I'd told my mother how two girls in my class kept talking about how amazing it was to confide in a therapist, she supported the idea and set up the appointment.

Elliot was more than six feet tall, with gray hair and stooped shoulders. I marveled at how long his arms and legs were as we sat across from each other. He always started the same way. "How has your week been going?"

Today was no different.

I rattled off the whole story, as if it had happened to somebody else. Elliot listened intently. When I finished he walked over to a file cabinet and pulled out an envelope. "This is a letter your mother wrote me," he said gently.

It was my mother's stationery, her name and address in blue print at the top. The letter was neatly typed, detailing all the issues regarding my anatomy.

"You knew too?"

He nodded. In his patient way he described how she had told him so he could help me, and asked him to wait until the diagnosis was definite before revealing that he knew.

He continued, "I wrestled with when to show you the letter. This was a hard choice for me, because it's not right for me to withhold information. But at the same time I didn't think I could do it before you found out. Your mother had been planning to tell you when all the information was gathered."

Now my feelings rushed in. "I'm so angry," I said and began to sob. Everything was a jumble. My mother just couldn't bear to tell me that now she had two handicapped daughters. She had given birth to two defective children. How could I be angry at her? But I wanted to punch her anyway. She may not have meant to betray me, but she had. Still, she'd gotten me a therapist, because she knew this would be horrible for me. In her own way, she was trying to help.

"This is a lot for you to take in," Elliot was saying, "but in time I will help you find your way through this."

I looked up and fumbled for the tissue box. With his long arm he reached for it and pulled one out for me.

Somewhere during that session he told me the story of how Floyd Patterson had lost a major fight because his beloved foster mother had just died. He spoke in a tender way about the many ways to be a parent.

"I can adopt," I said weeping.

"Of course," he said.

After the session I walked toward the subway still clutching the soggy tissue, my sweatshirt hood pulled tight. I had never even thought about having children, but now the desire was there in me, so strong and clear. Someday I would adopt. I had been thrown a life preserver.

A week after meeting the specialist, I sat next to my mother in another doctor's office. We'd had a big fight after I learned that in addition to my father, even my aunt knew of my condition. I told my mother I felt betrayed. She apologized, but couldn't explain why she hadn't even given me a hint about it earlier. I sort of understood; she hadn't known what to do. This reality was terrifying for us both, and suddenly I was glad she was with me.

The new doctor also had a mustache. He smiled at me, came from behind his desk to shake my hand, and then said "I'm Dr. Falk. Please sit down and let's have a talk."

I sat down in the chair next to him.

"I've looked over the report and I will examine you, but from what I see, it's true that you won't be getting a period. However," he paused, smiling, "there is another alternative to surgery. I know a kind of a peasant cure, but it takes a special kind of person who is willing to do some work. Perhaps you would like to try this," he said.

My shoulders hunched.

"I would give you a small glass tube, which you will lubricate and then slowly insert into your vagina, because you do have a small opening. You will gently push in and out against the muscle wall, and over time it will stretch. You'll have to do this every day for it to work. Periodically you will come back so I can evaluate. I will give you larger and larger tubes, and at some point when you have a boyfriend, you won't need to use the tube anymore. Your vagina will look and feel like any other woman's."

"And I can go to camp?" I said.

He assured me I could go, and it even sounded like I would end up normal.

"I would like to try."

"Let's begin now," he said, getting up and motioning me to follow him.

This time I only had to undress from the waist down. I climbed onto the examining table. I was freezing but not scared. Dr. Falk seemed like someone I could trust. I had no idea what was coming, but he'd told me I could go to camp.

He returned with a test tube, and then rubbed some clear goop called K-Y Jelly all over it until it got well lubricated. He told me to lie down and put my feet in the stirrups.

"Now I'm going to start using the tube. I'll begin gently, and then go farther in until you feel the pressure and it hurts a bit. When that happens, tell me right away. We need pressure, but we don't want it to hurt too much."

I closed my eyes and waited.

The suddenness of something cold and hard came pushing slowly into the edges of me. It was cold and greasy, but not too bad. I thought, I can take this, as I felt it pushing slowly inside. And then a little more, until it hit something hard in me, a piercing, hot moment of pain.

"It's hurting now," I screamed inside, but what came out of me was an unrecognizable high-pitched squeal. I opened my eyes, seeing only the whiteness of the doctor's lab coat.

"Okay, good girl, you did well. You can get dressed now. You're very brave. I want you to practice this for five minutes every day, and really push or it won't work. You have to get to the place where it just starts to hurt. This is not for everyone, and I want to know if you think you can do this."

"I can," I said.

I would do anything for it to work.

"Good," he said. "See you at the end of the summer."

I started practicing with the tube. Submerged under my quilt, sitting on my bed, I'd hold my breath and push, running to the bathroom afterward to wash myself and then scrub the jelly off the tube.

It amazes me now how I kept going with this painful process. I had suddenly been propelled into womanhood, forced to confront a reality that I was not remotely prepared for. I had never even been kissed, let alone had any thought of sexual intercourse. This practice was an insurance policy for some vague, unimaginable future. I think I got through it by focusing on pleasing the doctor. He had promised to help me be normal. I remember pushing and stretching and feeling proud of myself that I could stand it. But there was also a way in which I was dissociated. A tube was going in "down there," pushed by my hands, while my mind traveled elsewhere. Afterward, when I shoved the tube into my top drawer, it was as if I was trying to hide the whole experience.

What was left was a residue of inadequacy and shame.

I was damaged inside, all the more reason to work hard on my outer appearance.

One evening after finishing with the tube, I stood in front of the oval mirror over my dresser for another self-improvement project: setting my hair with plastic curlers. The first task was to isolate a small, even strand of hair, devilishly hard with my waves. When I found one, I pulled it straight and rolled it between the two prongs until it was tight against my head. After managing to use all the curlers, I looked in the mirror at my handiwork. Twigs of hair were sticking out in every direction. How to get this right was a mystery. Popular girls with mothers born in America knew how to do it, but my mother thought it was vulgar to see women with curlers and scarves wrapped around their heads on the street. She would never dream of setting her short hair, which she washed, dried with a towel and brushed behind her ears.

In a fit of anger, I pulled all the curlers out and banged my brush down on the dresser.

All of a sudden my father, holding his glasses, stood in the doorway. "What's going on?" he asked tenderly.

Tears welled up. "I can't set my hair," I said.

He came closer and picked up a curler. "Oh I see. How does this go?"

"Wow," I replied, embarrassed and surprised that he would be interested in me in this way. I could go to him for help with algebra, but not something that had to do with girl stuff.

"You're supposed to wrap your hair around these prongs really tight," I said, "and I can't do it."

"Like this?" he asked, lifting a hank of hair from the back and trying to roll it up.

I could feel his hands fumbling, and then dropping the curler. He was not someone who was good with his hands.

"Like that, but it's not easy," I said, so surprised that my shy father was actually trying this.

"I can see that," he said slowly, putting on his glasses, and again examining the uncooperative curler in his hand. "Let's try again."

"Okay," I said doubtfully. Still, I stood up straighter and held my breath. He grabbed some hair, rolled it very slowly around the curler, and snapped it closed.

We both stood back and looked in the mirror.

"It didn't work," he said.

"It doesn't matter." I pulled out the lopsided curler, feeling a rush of love for my father, who was willing to take this seriously and try to help me. "You did help. I can do the rest now."

He reached over to hug me. "You are Susie with the beautiful blue eyes." Then he repeated the family story about how when I was a little girl, a policeman had stopped us as we walked in the neighborhood to exclaim over my eyes. He was so proud of that.

My father and I had never spoken about my defect. If I had gotten my period, I doubt I would have shared that either.

But now we had had the deepest of conversations, wordlessly.

Chapter 9

After my difficult year, camp offered me a haven. But before I left, my mother gave me conflicting messages about how to take care of myself. On the one hand, she bought me a quilted bag for the tube and jelly, so that I would be organized and successful. On the other hand, she issued a warning. "Don't tell boys about you, because they might want to take advantage," she said.

In that one powerful sentence, she had communicated that I had something to hide, something wrong with me, and men were not to be trusted. Her warning fell so far from my innocent reality that I couldn't process it. I consciously dismissed it, yet felt shaky and off balance. Still, I stuffed the quilted bag into my duffel bag and, armed with my guitar case, climbed on the camp bus.

Looking back, I feel thankful for my willingness to venture forward in spite of everything, and for finding a glorious community that valued me and encouraged me to be myself.

As the bus pulled up a long gravel driveway, wooden cabins peeked out from the evergreens sloping up a gentle hill. When the bus door opened, a tall boy with dark curly hair jumped up the stairs and asked who needed help with luggage. As he moved down the aisle, I glimpsed his deep brown eyes and a dimpled smile, and our eyes locked. I felt chilled and hot at the same time. He was my ideal fantasy of handsome.

On that first evening as I stood awkwardly in front of the dining hall waiting for the dinner bell, I noticed him bent over doing something with his hands. Sidling over, I tried not to appear as if I were intentionally aiming for him. He looked up and waved. I walked closer and tried to smile, but thought for sure it looked more like a grimace.

"Have you ever seen a whittling knife?" he asked, opening his hand.

Whittling was not in my repertoire of conversation topics.

"I take a piece of wood and see what comes out of it. This one's going to be a dog," he explained, offering me a small piece of redwood that did look vaguely like an animal.

"Here, feel it." He put it in my hand.

"Wow, it's so smooth," I said, turning it over, holding back from saying, "Wow, you're so creative. You're amazing. Do you like me? I'm creative too. I'm so glad you're talking to me."

He introduced himself. All of a sudden Bob was the most beautiful of names. He had been a work camper last year, and this summer he was one of four paid staff assistants. I was still holding the piece of wood in my hand. Our counselors had mentioned that one of the ground rules for work campers was not dating counselors. Was he one?

The dinner bell rang. My fingers dropped the wood back into his hand without touching.

"Bring your guitar down to play before dinner sometime. We always have singing then," he offered, shoving the knife and wood back into his pocket.

That first week I caught glimpses of him through the trees. Once he even asked me how I was doing. And he always blushed when he saw me, so maybe that meant he liked me. I didn't know how to take the next step, but it came to me.

One dinner time 150 children of assorted ages jostled each other, shouting and elbowing one another to find a seat on the grassy area in front of the dining hall. Counselors were whistling and yelling, trying to get a head count for each bunk. My new friends and I were massaging each other's shoulders on the barn steps when I noticed that it was late and the music counselor hadn't yet arrived to lead the nightly singing. As that thought registered, I opened my guitar case and slung the green and white lanyard that held the instrument around my neck. I floated to the front of the group.

My left hand fingered the frets, as, in one confident swoop, my right hand slashed across the strings, vibrating into a gorgeous G major chord. "I'm going to lay down my sword and shield," I sang out, and clapping twice, pointed my guitar neck toward the group for them to respond just the way Pete Seeger did it. A moment's pause, "Down by the riverside," I sang, with two more claps. "Let's do it," I shouted. "Down by the riverside." Counselors started clapping, and I was nodding. "I can't hear you . . . Down by the riverside."

They were all singing and clapping in time to the music. I had them. I was out front leading the singing, and we were all joined together, words and music connecting us. I called out the next line and they called back. I was powerful, one with them but leading. Floating in the harmonies surrounding me on all sides, I could have kept going forever, but we were coming to the end of the song. One more chorus, one more "study war no more," the very last chord, and then that moment of silence when it all kept ringing inside. Followed by applause.

I looked up to see Bob smiling at me. My knees wobbled.

He walked over and put his hand on my shoulder. "You were great. Maybe you could show me some chords. I've always wanted to learn how to play."

"I would love to," I said.

Later that night I lay in bed, replaying the whole scene: being out in front of all those people, the glory of their response to my singing, and Bob admiring me. Yet, in the middle of that, I heard the echo of the doctor's voice, "No, you won't ever be able to have children."

There was something really wrong with me. The two doctors, my feet in the stirrups all came flooding back.

"No, it's okay," I told myself. "Not now. Don't think about it. Nothing is showing. You don't have to tell. And you will adopt children. People do that."

And then I flashed on Edna and me in our old apartment, holding hands, singing "Loch Lomond," and she was saying, "It's fine, Susie," and I was hugging her. That's the last moment I remembered.

The next day new busloads of children would arrive, but today we had the day off, and I was lying in a meadow under an endless blue sky with a boy. There was a faint scent of pine in the air. The grass felt soft and Bob plucked a long stem and grazed it down between my eyes and along my nose. I turned slowly to face him, and as I did the extra padding I had in my right bra cup popped up out of my shirt. In addition to all my other indignities, my right breast was smaller than my left. I stuffed it back down. Bob didn't say anything and I couldn't tell if he had noticed. He touched my face with his hand. I shivered a little.

"You have beautiful blue eyes," he said.

"I really like your brown ones," I replied.

I wished we would kiss, but he didn't move closer. Instead, he sat up and pulled his little redwood dog out of his shirt pocket.

"It's finished," he said, finding my hand and gently placing his creation in it.

"It's beautiful." I fingered the little uplifted tail and soft sway of the dog's back.

"We better head down. I have some chores," Bob said.

"Thank you for the present." I felt overwhelmed by his generosity, but confused by his sudden restlessness. "I really love it," I added.

"See you later," was all he said, grabbing my hand and squeezing it for a moment before running off.

So even though we hadn't kissed, I had my first boyfriend. My teen counselors had even met and decided to make an exception to the "no fraternizing with staff" rule for me, because they considered both of us to be responsible and mature. Our romance didn't have to be secret, and I was exuberant. For the first time in my life I was popular, in love, and a rule had even been stretched for me. And I loved being outdoors. Every morning I ran down the hill from our teen house, glimpsing the sun through the trees. I loved the eight-year-old girls picking up their dropped towels as they ran toward the pool. I straightened out knots in their lanyards at craft time, hoping for a glimpse of Bob. In the afternoon, I stood on a ladder painting a woodland mural on the outside wall of the library, hoping he would see me, as I stretched to reach the top of the painting.

Everything was perfect.

Still, there was my tube secreted away in the quilted pink pouch. Simple. Take it into the bathroom after evening activity before anyone else came in. Duck into the stall and smear on the jelly. Stick it inside me. Sometimes it's cold, but don't think about that. Just do it. If someone comes in, stick it back in the bag and wash it out tomorrow when no one would see. You can do this.

Chapter 10

Camp was over, but Bob was still my boyfriend. He called and said *yes* when I invited him over for dinner.

When he arrived, my mother did a double take, and I could tell she thought he was handsome. I couldn't wait to be alone with him, but first we had to get through eating cold chicken breast at the picnic table.

Soon after Bob passed the respectability test, my parents disappeared. We went out into the backyard and lay down in the grass. The shadow of the Japanese maple tree was fading into the darkness of a warm late summer night. We lay facing each other and began to kiss softly. But then Bob rolled over onto his back and began looking up at the night sky.

I reached over and put my arm across his chest, and gently slid my hand under his shirt. Then I raised myself up on my other hand and, without thinking, inched on top of him. In the darkness, I dared to want more. We lay there for a long minute without moving.

"It's getting to be time to leave," he said, gesturing me off with his shoulder.

Something was amiss, but all I could do was scramble up.

He left by the side yard without going back into the house.

All the next week I waited for him to call before finally dialing his number. His mother answered. He was busy getting ready for college, she explained, but she would let him know I'd called. After three weeks I sent him a card with a picture of a forest on the front, and wrote, "Just wondering how you're doing."

I never heard back.

I replayed the scene over and over, and poured my suffering into a poem called "Summer Love," which got published in my school literary magazine. Important people in my class complimented me. This was a victory, but didn't help to change the fact that I had been tossed back into the defective pile. And now I was not only physically disabled, but my forwardness and desire for physical closeness was an added defect. I had scared him off. Rather than seeing him as uptight or possibly gay—a thought that never would have occurred to me then—I believed I had been too eager. A proper girl would have played hard to get.

But even though I felt hopeless, I persisted with the tube, my daily payment on the insurance policy for a future normal body.

"Looking good," Dr. Falk said. "Time for a larger one. And one other thing." He cleared his throat and cleared it again. "Ummm, when you're working with the tube, do you ever feel anything else, like tingling maybe?"

What a dumb question. I knew what he meant. Why did he want to know that? For the first time, I felt embarrassed in front of him.

"No," I answered, my eyes shut tight.

He reassured me that everything was fine and I should get dressed. But later in bed I felt weird. Using the tube was a medical procedure that I endured by putting it in its own compartment and distancing myself from it. It had nothing to do with how I felt warm and open lying on the grass with Bob. The doctor had been gentle when he asked, but I'd felt squeamish inside. Exploring my sexuality in that context was simply impossible.

It's miraculous to me now that when I began to be sexual with men, I was able to feel passionate. The fact that I didn't have to worry about getting pregnant the way my friends did gave me the freedom to explore and enjoy myself. But at the time, all I could do was dissociate in difficult situations.

Which played a big role in my next foray into dating. I was about to go on my first blind date with Jonathan, a camp friend's brother who was coming home from college for spring break.

When the bell rang that Friday promptly at six, my parents were seated on the couch. They had insisted on meeting Jonathan. Running to open the door, I pulled my tight, black V-neck sweater down to reveal as much cleavage as possible. He was slender with blue eyes, and he had an orange-and-black-striped scarf artfully draped around his neck so that one end was a bit longer than the other.

Preppy looking, not my type. I preferred a scruffier, earnest folk singer look.

Jonathan flashed me a wink and slid past me. Aiming directly for my father, he smiled and thrust his arm out at him.

My father hesitated, but stood up and took his hand.

"You have such a lovely home. Who plays the piano?" Jonathan asked, and without pausing, he walked over and ran his hand over some of the keys of the open baby grand.

I could tell my mother was uncomfortable.

"Pleasure to meet you, too," Jonathan quickly said to her.

"I think we should be going." I grabbed my pea coat from the closet.

"So we're off to the city to get some dinner," he told my parents on our way out.

When we got on the train, he reached over and took my hand. My legs in new stockings were squeezed together, careful to avoid his. I nodded as he told me he was not pledging a frat, was majoring in sociology, and was planning to go to graduate school. For a second I noticed that he asked nothing about me, but mostly I focused on trying to smile.

At Times Square he nudged me out of the subway car, telling me this would be a good stop, and as we walked down Forty-Second Street, he put his arm around me.

"How about a steak?" he said, "Tad's is pretty good, and it's right on the next block."

Peering through the bright red-and-orange flames painted on the window, I could see a skinny man wearing an apron stained with charcoal and ketchup blobs flipping greasy-looking pieces of meat on a grill. It looked so dinky. I told myself that maybe going to this type of place was some kind of cool college thing to do.

After Jonathan ordered his steak well done, I expressed my preference for medium rare. When the two steaks came, there was no difference between them. As I chewed the toughest meat I had ever tasted, he told me he was an atheist. I wondered if he thought I was pretty.

After Tad's we wandered around Times Square, seemingly with no particular destination. It was freezing out. I buttoned my coat, and when he put his arm around me again, my shoulders tightened up. We passed by a doorway with a red neon sign blinking "HOTEL." He pulled me closer and steered me back to it. We stood for a moment and, without saying a word, he pushed the door open. My brain was not computing anything, but my body sensed something ominous. And then I left myself. From a distance, I watched myself walking into a hotel. Pungent smell of pine cleanser stung my nostrils. Scratched red-and-black linoleum squares on the floor. Room empty except for a registration desk, made of some kind of fake cracked marble. Jonathan's arm still around me, I was led to the desk. A man with dandruff on his eyebrows and gray stringy hair arranged to hide his baldness was huddled over a newspaper. *The New York Daily News.*

"We'd like a room for two."

Jonathan's voice echoed inside me. I heard the words and knew that they meant we would go into a room with nothing but a big bed in it. From my out-of-body perch, I saw a young man talking to the desk clerk about a room. There was a mute girl standing next to him.

The clerk looked up from his paper and slowly pushed his glasses down over his nose. He peered at me, then at Jonathan, and then back at me.

"I don't think so," he said. "She's too young."

I registered that to mean we wouldn't be going up in the elevator, which I was just noticing.

"No," he said again, fixing his eyes on Jonathan. "Definitely not."

At that moment I came back to myself. What was I doing here? Jonathan's face was turning blotchy red, like the bloody apron at Tad's. I looked at the man, who stared at me and then turned back to his newspaper. A ripple of fear ran through me. Something really bad had almost happened. And then another glimmer of a thought. This creepy-looking man had helped me. He didn't have to, but he did. And now I didn't have to do this sinister, skin-crawly thing.

Without a word, Jonathan turned me around, and we walked out of the hotel.

In a fog, aware that his arm was still around me, I heard him say it was getting late. We hurtled down the subway stairs. Once on the train I made sure no part of me was touching any part of him.

The train pulled into my stop. I jumped away from him and ran up the stairs. He was right behind me. Running toward the token booth, I saw my father pacing back and forth in his old rawhide moccasin slippers, his pajama bottoms sticking out from under his coat. As our eyes met, I saw a frantic wildness in his I had never seen before. He began waving his arms, motioning to me.

"*Gott sei dank*, there you are," he said, the moment I reached the stairs.

"What are you doing here?" I asked, beginning to sob.

"It's very late," was all he said.

He motioned Jonathan away, grabbed my hand and pulled me up the stairs to the street.

"Why did you come?" I asked.

"Your mother and I had a funny feeling about him, and when you were late, I got worried."

"You were right," I said.

He looped his arm in mine, and all the way up the hill to our house, I kept my hand in the pocket of his warm wool coat.

Just as I anticipated going away to college, my mother's warning had come true. Even without sharing my secret with Bob or Jonathan, I was unacceptable date material and boys would try to take advantage of me.

Chapter 11

The gap between Edna and me widened when I left home for SUNY Binghamton. Away from my parents, I could ignore their worries about how Edna wasn't fitting in to her school. Apparently, the other children didn't remind the teachers about activities that they forgot, but Edna did. And her motor issues complicated her ability to learn to write with a pencil and throw a ball. The school just didn't seem right for her.

But I was immersed in my own difficulties: How much time to spend in the library reading Plato? Should I sneak out of the dorm after our 10:30 weekday curfew to go drinking? I did and got caught trying to get back in, and was put on social probation for a semester. More concerning was my ever-present secret. It was easy enough to use the tube when my roommate was out or up early for a class. But without the friends I would later confide in, I was wrapped in a stoic loneliness that I wasn't really aware of.

About that, one memory stands out.

On a late autumn evening, I trundled into my room after spending hours at the library, working on a lit paper that was due the next morning. Girls were sprawled over the two twin beds discussing their latest dates. Making room for me on my madras spread, I lay over the bed with my head hanging down toward the floor. I'd had some first dates, but nobody I wanted to kiss.

I began to unpin the metal hairpins in my long hair to release the bun I wore when I hadn't washed it. I was twirling a hairpin when the conversation veered into Tampax. Everyone laughed at the story of how one fell out of someone's purse while she was searching for a cigarette on a date. I had never held a Tampax, let alone imagined carrying one in my purse. Maybe I should buy a package to see what they were like. Then I could be part of the conversation. Next the topic switched to diaphragms. One girl's older sister had one and had showed her how to insert it. As she began to describe the process, I stared at the hairpin until I dissolved into blankness. With the hairpin in my fingers, my head sank lower toward the floor. I noticed a wall socket. As if I was computing some logical equation, I remember looking at the hairpin and saying to myself: "Two prongs, and two holes in the socket, they fit," just before jamming them into the holes.

Hearing a scream, I stared up at my roommate's concerned face.

"I can't believe what I just did. Don't know what I was thinking," I said. "The shock wasn't too bad. Really, I'm okay."

But I knew exactly what I had been thinking.

I hated this secret. I hated myself.

And then there was big news.

Seemingly out of nowhere, an opportunity had materialized for Edna. It was a possibility so out of the realm of our lives that it could have been launched from the moon. A friend of a distant cousin with an autistic son about Edna's age had learned of Camphill Village, a newly forming spiritual community in upstate New York. Based on the teachings of Rudolph Steiner, an esoteric Viennese philosopher who was a contemporary of Freud's, it was to be an intentional community *with*, not for, mentally handicapped adults.

This information was dropped during a Sunday night phone call home. My mother excitedly told me this could be the start of a whole new life for Edna. Handicapped people could be spiritual teachers for normal people, or "coworkers," as they were called. My father told me he knew of Steiner's philosophy, called Anthroposophy, from Germany. It included elements of Christianity and Eastern thought, such as reincarnation. With the specter of institutions still haunting my parents, this seemed like manna from heaven.

It sounded crazy to me. Maybe my parents were clutching at straws? I wanted to protect them from disappointment. I told them the place sounded really weird and maybe they should find out more about it. They answered that we were all going to visit during my winter break, and we could talk then. I couldn't begin to imagine Edna living in some far out, off-the-grid farm.

The day was cold and foggy as we crawled up the Taconic State Parkway. Edna and I sat holding hands in the back seat of our secondhand Nash Rambler. My father kept glancing at his watch. For him being late was a moral lapse, and we were now past the two hours it was supposed to take to get there. Edna started to sing, "Make new friends and keep the old." My mother and I chimed in for several rounds, until finally we all fell silent. The *thunk* of the windshield wipers put me into a trance. Edna's eyes closed and her head fell over onto my shoulder. My mother rummaged in her briefcase that held my sister's psychological tests, along with the physical and occupational therapy reports that were supposed to explain Edna, while my father gripped the steering wheel tightly with both hands. Finally, he turned off the highway and then onto a rutted dirt road. We lurched past a faded red barn.

"We're here," my mother said, pointing to the neat, hand-painted sign next to the barn.

"Camphill Village," Edna read. "Will they have cows?"

I rubbed the window with my sleeve to see out the window and noticed several cow pies near the fence. Maybe the farm thing would be good for Edna.

Someone was waving to us from a newly painted frame house.

My mother sat up straighter and searched in her briefcase for a pocket comb, as my father walked around the car checking how deep the tires had sunk in the mud.

But Edna, coat open, boots squeaking through the mud, was already hurtling toward the door. My mother, briefcase and mouth set tight, followed. I hung back, but my father took my arm and we walked together.

"I'm Edna Wile and I was on a farm when I was younger," Edna said to the serious looking, bearded man who opened the door.

I immediately lapsed into my nine-year-old squirmy self and wished I weren't here.

But the man matched her with, "I'm Carlo Piezner and that's wonderful. Please come in."

We filed past him into a room with Danish chairs and a low wooden coffee table piled with books. I noticed amethyst rock crystals, a candle, and a curved metal candle-snuffer arranged on a multicolored scarf on the table. Next to that, a photograph of a man with dark bugging-out eyes peered out of a pentagonal wooden frame, which was beveled so there were no right angles. This had to be Rudolf Steiner. That display, I concluded, must be the spiritual part.

Edna sat down on the couch between my parents, and I lowered myself into the chair farthest away.

A tall, angular woman appeared in the doorway carrying a tea tray with cups and cookies. Her long skirt, loose turtleneck and Norwegian sweater looked faded and drab. Yet she had style. A purple tie-dyed scarf was loosely folded around her neck, pinned with a simple silver brooch. There was a gracefulness in the way she moved across the room and set down the tray, all in one motion.

"Hello to you," she said reaching out her hand. Her blue eyes had a clear openness. And something else: a kind of going inward at the same time as she looked at me. I felt drawn to her.

"And you are?" she continued.

"Edna's sister."

"Ah, yes," she said, looking at me intently. "That's fine."

I felt her take me in and then again, that going inward. What was that? A kind of light from her when she did that. And when she told me her name was Renata, she trilled her R's in a gentle and flowing way. Hers was a German accent, but a softer one than I was used to. And there was something very different about the way she just seemed to be, with both an intensity and a calmness I had never encountered.

She turned, walked over to Edna, shook her hand, and said, "You are Edna, and I have been waiting to meet you."

All of a sudden, I felt comfortable.

Carlo was explaining that there were ten villagers living at Camphill already, and several "coworkers" had arrived from England and Denmark. These people had all lived in similar villages in Europe and were committed to creating this one. He asked Edna to tell him what she liked to do.

"I like singing with my sister, playing records, and being on a farm." Then she picked up a lumpy, homemade-looking cookie and tried to bite into it. "This is good," she said.

I took one, too. It was as hard as a rock.

When Renata suggested to Edna that they take a walk to look around, Edna's face lit up.

While she and Renata were off on their tour, I found myself drifting in and out, picking up bits of the conversation. Carlo explained that an essential part of the community's philosophy was that everyone worked. They already had the farm, gardens, and a doll-making shop.

"But Edna is not good with her hands," my mother said.

Carlo assured her that there was something for everyone, even if it was setting the table, chopping vegetables, or sweeping after lunch. Each villager went out to work in a house different from the one in which they lived.

From the corner of my eye I watched my father with his furrowed brow listening intently. "And the coworkers, who are they, and how do they come here? How can this all work financially?" he asked.

Carlo explained that the coworkers choose to live with villagers as part of their spiritual path. They were called coworkers, rather than staff, because Camphill was their home, too. They were not paid, but all their needs were met. Growing up with Edna, I'd had to deal with her challenges and had benefited from it. But choosing to live with a whole bunch of handicapped people was unfathomable to me.

My mother opened her briefcase and announced that she had all of Edna's reports.

"They won't be necessary," Carlo said.

"Why not?"

"I can see already that Edna would be good for the village."

"So you don't need to see anything?" my mother asked, her voice incredulous.

Carlo shook his head. My parents turned toward each other for the first time that day, staring in disbelief. That one sentence had just transformed the landscape of our lives. In that moment, I knew Edna was going to live here.

Nobody had ever said that Edna would be good for anything, or that people would voluntarily choose to live with her.

Just then, Edna and Renata returned from their walk.

"All the cows have names and they are written on their stalls," Edna told us." And we milk them by hand, like Floyd did on the farm."

She was standing without her usual hunched shoulders. Had I never noticed what a lovely slim figure she had? She had been an adorable roly-poly child, but now I was looking at a shapely seventeen-year-old with long lashes and shining blue eyes. And then I realized she had said, "*We* milk them by hand."

She was already living there. Edna had found her home.

Without complaining, she had endured the trials of two boarding schools where she didn't fit in. Having experienced the village, she immediately grasped the difference and wholeheartedly embraced her new path. I could say I felt moved and inspired, but it was much more than that. I felt awe. Edna's joy was medicine for me.

CHAPTER 12

EDNA AND I were both young women exploring new worlds, but in my mind she remained a child. I thought of my struggles as occurring in the "real world," while she was living in a protected community. Yet she was a pioneer, one of the first eleven villagers—as the handicapped people were called—to join Camphill. She was busy learning her job, which was preparing second breakfast for those in the doll-making workshop. She read Bible stories every Saturday evening, and generally was learning to navigate the challenges of living with a coworker family that included a newborn, as well as several other villagers. When I visited, I was drawn into the slow-paced, otherworldly feeling of the village. I recognized Edna's accomplishments. Still, back at college, her world was so hard to explain that I found myself keeping her in a separate compartment as I forged ahead with my studies and making new friends.

One afternoon in the student center snack bar, I dared myself to sit with some of the cool, beatnik-looking upperclassmen. Deep in a conversation about early American metaphysical poetry, nobody acknowledged my presence. Someone mentioned Edward Taylor. Remembering him from my high school AP class I took the leap.

"Didn't he write a poem with the metaphor of a spinning wheel?" I asked.

"How would you know?" a boy in a scratched up leather jacket asked in a condescending tone, staring at me through thick glasses.

"Just remembered it, not sure how," I said, excited to be noticed.

The conversation continued as if I weren't there. I slid out of my chair and lifted it to make no noise as I slid it back in, and then crept away.

A week later, walking through the student center, I felt someone deliberately bump into me. I looked up to see the boy in the scratched leather jacket.

"I thought you might like this," he said, handing me a new hard-cover book.

I stared down at ee cummings's collected poems, but before I could thank him, he loped away into the crowd.

I opened the book. Inside it in tiny, neat handwriting was the inscription "and flowers pick themselves," followed by a page number. I ran my fingers over the inscription, staring at every curve of it, before finding the page and jumping to the last phrase: "where/ always/ it's Spring) and everyone's/ in love and flowers pick themselves." I had just received my first important gift from a man: an inscribed book of poetry that spoke of love.

The next afternoon, while sitting in the student center trying not to devour a toasted English muffin dripping with butter, I spotted him sauntering toward me. My heart jumped.

"Your poem in the literary magazine is good," he said, sitting down.

"You know who I am?" I said, surprised.

"Obviously," he replied, introducing himself. "Arthur."

Stammering, I told him how much I loved ee cummings.

He nodded and, without acknowledging my comment, mentioned that his friends on the lit mag were going to hang out at his off-campus apartment and I could drop by. He wrote down his address and told me the bus stopped a block away. But before I could collect myself, he walked away. He seemed to have perfected this jackrabbit way of popping up and disappearing.

From a sagging wooden porch, I entered a darkened living room with empty beer bottles lined up along the length of an entire wall. A lanky, painfully thin guy with carrot-red hair curling around his neck was emerging from a back bedroom, one arm around a large-bosomed girl in a barely-tied bathrobe. I knew immediately who he was: a legendary campus poet. He gave me a nod as he passed. Without getting up, Arthur waved me in. Among the many six packs on the table, I could choose between beer and ale. I didn't know what ale was. A gnome-like girl raised her head from a book of Rilke's poems to explain that ale was stronger than beer. Choosing beer, I sat in a scratchy, stained armchair and crossed my legs. Arthur and the gnome girl seemed to be matching each other's grimacing faces, in between swigs of beer.

I was reaching for a second one when Arthur swiveled toward me, and said, "You should definitely take Hagopian's Chaucer class. The journey theme, good stuff."

"See you soon," was his only other comment, as I piled into a car with other girls to make it back to the dorm before curfew.

A week later, when Arthur approached me in the library, he suggested taking a walk. He grabbed my hand and steered me down one of the cement walkways. When we got to the end of it, he put his arm around me and we began walking through brush up a hill. I could see wooded hills in the distance. It was a cold, early spring day, with trees radiating a readiness that promised buds and leaves. I pulled my turtleneck up over my chin and buttoned my pea coat as we entered thicker woods with taller trees.

After ten minutes of walking in silence, Arthur swept some branches away, revealing a large tree with a thick overhang of branches. "We're here," he said.

I followed the upward motion of his arm and made out a crude platform with branches full of buds bending over it.

"It's the tree house," he announced, sweeping his hand across the length of it.

"This is fantastic, did you build this?" I asked.

"Yup, with help from four people. Took us a weekend. It's only a very select group of people who are allowed here." He gave me a leg up, and then hoisted himself up. We sat dangling our legs over the edge of the plywood platform that was nailed to logs. Beyond the tangle of branches I saw puffy clouds and a scrap of blue sky.

I shivered, and he put his arm around me, pulled me close, and suddenly we were kissing. First a few gentle ones, and then his tongue found its way into my mouth. My eyes were closed. I felt him stretch out on his back and pull me on top of him. I could feel his hardness through our jeans. I knew what it was, but it was the first time I'd ever felt it. I began rocking over it, up, down, and sideways. Both of us were breathing hard. No hands touched any part of each other. We were just jacketed bodies. Sharp sensations were pitching inside me. No control, just a flooding. A sudden *whoosh* and it was over. My first orgasm. Wild and astonishing that it had happened. And that it had happened outside in the woods, really hip. But mainly so amazing that Dr. Falk was right, that in this way I was normal. He had told me this during my first visit with him, but back then it was all a blur, not something I could begin to understand. But now I did. I could do this, I could feel this, and nobody could ever take it away from me.

Arthur and I slipped into being a couple. At night he walked me to my dorm after being together in the library. He advised me which classes to take next semester, and his friends now made room for me at the snack bar table. We spent hours at the tree house, never undressing or going all the way. My secret was safe for now. I loved his intelligence and offbeat cynical humor. He loved Coney Island, Nathan's hot dogs, and his Yiddish-speaking grandmother, and was planning to introduce me to all of them during spring break. Everything felt exotic to me.

On our first spring break afternoon, we were naked in a twin bed in Brooklyn. Arthur had taken me home to meet his family, but they had all gone out, and we lay under his brown plaid quilt. Without my glasses, the room was an impressionist painting: brown blur of quilt, light coming through the blinds, plain beige walls, and Arthur's blue eyes. We were on our sides, facing each other. He was much thinner than I'd thought, having only felt him through his clothing. He began to touch my breasts. I felt shy to touch him. He maneuvered me onto my back and began to climb on top of me. I wanted what was coming, but I hadn't yet told him about me. What if he could tell there was something weird about my anatomy? We hadn't even discussed going all the way. Maybe he would bring up condoms now. But he didn't. Shouldn't he be doing that? But then he was on top of me, starting to move.

"Hold on, I have to put my diaphragm in," I said, in a sudden burst of inventiveness.

I jumped up, grabbed my Fred Braun brown leather pocketbook, and began rummaging through it.

"Right back," I whispered.

Shutting the bathroom door, naked in a strange bathroom facing terry cloth bathrobes hanging on a hook, I lowered myself onto the toilet seat. Figuring it would take at least a minute to put a diaphragm in, I counted to sixty. Imagining that someone would wash their hands after inserting it, I ran the sink tap.

"All done," I said, as he lifted the quilt and I crawled back in, hoping he wouldn't be able to feel anything unusual.

He pulled the hairpins out of my bun, and my hair brushed his chest.

I was starting to relax and feel excited.

"I love your blue eyes," he said as he moved on top of me.

Closing them, I felt him sliding into me. It was working; we were moving together.

We came at the same time. I opened my eyes searching his to see if he thought there was anything unusual about me. He smiled and stroked my hair. Everything was okay. I was okay, officially a woman, a sexual woman who had just made love for the first time.

I had just cashed in my tube policy.

A week later we were sitting together on the grass near the student center when I mentioned there was something I needed to tell him. I took his hand and began by saying there was something different about me. He nodded and waited.

"I wasn't sure when to say this, but here goes. The thing is, I don't menstruate," I said searching his face for clues that whatever it was, he would still love me.

He was his usual impassive self.

I paused again, searching his face, but then rushed on. "I do ovulate, but the eggs go directly into my bloodstream because I don't have a uterus."

"Okay," he said, tilting his face up toward me, as if asking a question.

I understood that he was wondering how that would affect him.

I could feel myself distancing from myself as I continued. "So I can't give birth to my own children. I would want to adopt though. Not that we are in that place, I get that, but I just wanted you to know." Now it was my turn to wait. I picked some grass with my free hand and blew it into the air.

"I'm fine with that. Doesn't make any difference to me," he said, after a while. "How do you know all this?"

I briefly recounted my visit to the doctor, leaving out the part about the tube. No need to spill it all right now.

He squeezed my hand. "Never heard of anything like that. But really glad you told me. Let's get lunch."

Until I made love, I had never actually imagined telling my story to a boy. All these years my fear of rejection had lived in me as an inchoate field of anxiety. Now I had a boyfriend who accepted me. It could have been a moment of joy, release, maybe even with sadness mixed in. But, strangely, I wasn't feeling much of anything except relief that I didn't have to worry about when I would tell him.

I think now that was partially because Arthur had difficulty being emotionally responsive. And in a deeper way, I still felt damaged inside. Yet, I had begun to feel that I passed for normal in the sexual sphere. How I had gotten there was nobody's business. And we were so young that the issue of children was abstract and irrelevant. I had just postponed that reckoning.

CHAPTER 13

AT THE END of my sophomore year, if a fortune-teller had told me that I would marry Arthur one year later, I would have been incredulous. He was graduating and heading to the Peace Corps, an acceptable way to avoid the draft. It was understood that our lives would unfold separately, and there was no talk of remaining committed to each other.

I hadn't meant to continue as Arthur's girlfriend. Thinking of him far away in Africa had been a secret relief. He hadn't been terribly affectionate when we were alone, and in public we never walked arm in arm. Even at the movies, he never put his arm around me. A surreptitious squeeze of my hand was the best I could hope for. In his odd way I knew Arthur cared about me, but I sensed something was missing.

But then at the last minute something went awry, and the Peace Corps rejected him. Having done that, and aware of his draft status, they arranged for him to go to graduate school in Florida for a one-year master's degree program as a stopgap. When I started my junior year, Arthur began graduate school.

So there we were, on a Friday night in November of my junior year in 1963, sitting next to each other on a bed in a darkened motel room in Washington, DC. I'd been excited when he'd called to suggest meeting in the middle for a rendezvous, and had flown down to meet him. We lay next to each other as he prattled on about brewing beer in his bathtub. We had made perfunctory love. I felt deflated.

I heard a pause after the beer recipe, and in the same tone of voice he continued, "Hey, kiddo, I was thinking, why don't we get married next summer?"

I tried to rouse myself. Could he really be saying that?

He was looking down at the floor. "I'll have my degree, and I could come back to Binghamton and get a job teaching, and you could finish school. What do you think?"

Why? What? No, God no, not what I want, an inner scream went off deep inside of me.

"Look it's not just about how being married will get me a deferment."

My mind was working at a furious pace. He still thinks of me as his girlfriend, he needs my help. We had never actually broken up. Maybe I needed him too. Graduate school was a draft deferment that was ending. We had never actually discussed it, but at some point he had made a joke about how getting married was a way out of the draft. At the time, I had totally put it out of my mind. Still, I didn't want him to be drafted, and I tried to convince myself that I probably would end up marrying him anyway. Back at school, I was pretty sure that the guy I had a crush on now would go back to his old girlfriend. That relationship was pure fantasy and this was real. Don't listen to the *no*, I told myself, and all would be fine.

I heard myself say, "Yes. Yes, let's do that."

On an August afternoon ten days before my twentieth birthday, my parents threw a wedding with a tent in the backyard of our house in Queens. I wore sandals and an ankle-length white eyelet dress to stand in front of the rabbi we'd met five minutes before the ceremony. Being super cool, we had no aisle or bridesmaids, and instead of a shower, my friends had literally thrown me into one. But they were all there crowding around me as we said our vows, and Arthur stepped on the light bulb wrapped in a napkin.

I was going through with it, even though I felt disconnected. I concentrated on the details, such as the pretty pink piece of ribbon that threaded through my dress, the bubbles in the champagne glass, and how the rabbi had such a thick Brooklyn accent I couldn't tell when his Hebrew switched to English. And I kept my eyes on Edna.

"I'm Susan's sister," she said to anyone who would listen.

My friends were polite, but I could see them backing off. Arthur's grandma helped Edna fill her plate at the buffet table and sat next to her at dinner.

"I live at Camphill Village," I heard her say, as I flitted by.

I thanked Grandma in my heart.

And it was fine, just as I had told myself. Marrying Arthur was a perfect storm of inner and outer forces that converged. Saving him from being drafted into the Vietnam War was a powerful reason, but not enough on its own. The human psyche has its own logic, one that seeks to protect and keep us safe. Marrying Arthur, I had rationalized, would protect me from ever having to risk rejection and shame from telling other men about my body. His acceptance had granted me the status of normality, and I relished it.

We went back to Binghamton for my senior year, and lived off campus on a narrow back street in a second floor apartment. Sadie, our eighty-year-old Polish landlady, would leave plates of butter-soaked homemade pierogies in front of our door. I played house. My jealous friends who were still living in the dorms received invitations for dinners of chicken with almonds in white wine. We drank beer, listened to the Beatles, and I bustled around clearing away empty cans.

But then there was the matter of the twin beds. Arthur had

convinced me they were cool, that in some kind of retro chic way we would be parodying our parents. I went along with it, but then that seemed to go with sex only every two or three weeks. That didn't feel right.

One winter night I woke up, sat bolt upright in my twin bed and said to myself, "I'm going to die without ever having slept with anyone else." I'd never had that thought before. But there it was, fully formed and reverberating throughout my body and soul. And in the next moment I got very clear that I couldn't live my whole life without other experiences of making love. A nearly sexless marriage couldn't be all there was. That one sentence embodied worlds I couldn't have articulated at the time: that I was entitled to something deeper and more passionate, that I had been replicating my parents' sexless marriage, and that I had cheated on myself, suppressing my needs before I'd even gotten started. I had no clue as to how I would accomplish my revelation. But this geyser of yearning to feel more fully alive, rushing up from the deepest place in me, wasn't going to stop.

I lay back down and fell into a deep sleep.

Chapter 14

My plan was to sleep with someone, get it out of my system, and stay married.

A couple of weeks after my nighttime insight, I downed two beers at an off-campus party and found Dave, a BMOC (Big Man on Campus), leaning against the kitchen sink. He wore jeans and a suede vest over a loose turtleneck, and his wavy, unruly, dirty blond hair cascaded over his forehead. He was my picture of sexy.

Looking him straight in the eyes, I said, "Hey Dave, listen, if you don't ask me any questions and you keep this between us, I'd like to come over to your apartment some night." My eyes held his.

Registering no surprise, he looked down at the beer in his hands, as he massaged it with his thumbs. "That could happen," he answered, a slow grin spreading across his face. "Yeah, that could happen."

But that one night wasn't enough, and so there was another and then another. I kept telling myself everything was now fine. But more questions kept coming. Why didn't Arthur want to be more sexual? Why did he seem perfectly happy with this arrangement? Why didn't he notice when I put on one of the nightgowns I had received as a wedding present? Always tired from getting up early to teach, he was often asleep by eight, while I lay in bed burning up. I was afraid to tell him what had happened or to ask for more. In his way, he was devoted to me, building a couch for our living room and writing me parodies of Heloise's Helpful Household Hints. And he had been so accepting about not having our own children.

For the next four years I experimented with other casual, and even a few longer-term affairs, until finally I understood that I would never get the kind of love I needed from my flings. And though it terrified me to abandon the security and comfort I had with Arthur, it was scarier still to imagine staying in my marriage. It wasn't clear how my future would turn out, but I had to break free.

Arthur and I had moved from Binghamton to Brooklyn for my first year of graduate social work school. And so the following summer, I moved into a tiny studio apartment on the Upper West Side of Manhattan, furnished with a bed, low table, candles, incense, and fantasies. At twenty-three, when some of my college friends were getting engaged, I announced my divorce.

When I reflect on that time in my life, I see a conflicted young woman, desperately searching for acceptability through a fifties-style conventional marriage, while also seeking new experiences and great passion—two incompatible drives.

With my divorce in 1968, I was thrust into the arena of free love, experimentation with drugs, and the nascent Women's Liberation Movement. My body was made for the sixties hippie era: I couldn't have children, but was free to enjoy sex without worrying about getting pregnant. "It's my booby prize," I joked to my new friends in a consciousness-raising group when I told them about my anatomy.

I don't know if it was fully conscious then, but it's clear to me now that I often made light of my sense of feeling damaged as a way to minimize how much it dominated my psyche. At the time, it felt powerful and radical to engage with other women as we came to realize the degree to which we made men the center of our lives, to the detriment of appreciating ourselves. But that was so much easier to contemplate than to change the complex reality of my life.

The naïve assumption I worked from flowed right out of the sixties ethos, summed up in the Beatles song, "All You Need Is Love." My personal translation was that becoming a femme fatale might make up for my other deficiencies. That, in turn, led to my becoming sexual early on in any relationship, which usually backfired. In the back of my mind, I sensed this wasn't always the right strategy, but my anxiety and craving for love often overcame my better judgment. I got caught in a web of sleeping with a man to soothe and bolster my ego, but when I didn't hear from him, I became anxious. Which led to a merry-go-round of repeated behavior. Every one-night stand was the date that could lead to a fulfilling relationship. Wouldn't one of these men realize how sweet and capable I was? Besides, weren't women who didn't sleep with men right away prudes? Yet, those prudes seemed to snag husbands, while I found myself alone with my incense.

Not without a sense of humor, I once began a limerick about a doctor whom I dated briefly: "There once was a urologist from Iraq/ who promised that he would call back."

I managed to hang on to one relationship for several months, but most of my twenties were spent on a stream of stop-and-go encounters, tempered by good women friends and building my career as a therapist.

Unlike me, at Camphill Edna was shielded from the sex and drugs aspects of the sixties. Still, her back-to-the-land, spiritually oriented community embraced many other emerging ideas of the times. For example, the village farmed in a biodynamic way, baked its own bread, and hand-dipped candles. Rather than seeing Camphill as a weird place to avoid, I became increasingly open to its beauty. And instead of tagging along with my parents, I felt drawn to visit on my own, sometimes even staying overnight in Edna's house.

"I'm Edna's sister," I would announce to each villager I met. It was as Edna's sister that I was welcomed—a new, positive identity that I was proud of.

That she had a rich life and we were able to connect in her world represented a powerful shift in attitude for me. The minute I drove into the village, I felt myself breathe more easily in this stigma-free environment. And because the village was expanding, I always found myself wondering what new garden or festival was being planned. I no longer had to protect Edna, nor did I feel shame around her. More often, my visits were about *poor me*, and whatever storm I was embroiled in.

An unexpected bounty was meeting other siblings, exchanging phone numbers, and going out to lunch with our villagers. We even shared our feelings at a siblings' workshop the village offered. Never having met other siblings of disabled people, I was both startled and relieved to realize that most of us had assumed parental caretaking roles with our sisters and brothers. Many of us also had chosen to work in the helping professions. In the workshop, we discussed our longing to shed our role as a surrogate parent and explore what it would be like to be just a sibling. The most important outcome was our universal desire to have more fun with them. So, we created "Brother and Sister Day," an annual picnic to hang out the way normal siblings did. We spread madras bedspreads on the grass, grilled hot dogs, and played catch with an easy-to-retrieve beach ball.

"This is my sister Susan," Edna said excitedly, introducing me to every villager and coworker.

I saw Sarah, with whom I had worked closely in planning the event, pouring lemonade for her sister Patty. Sarah and I hugged and clinked glasses.

"I'm loving this," she said.

"The first of many," I replied.

"We got a good turnout, but there are a bunch missing," she added.

As if on cue, Alan, a tall villager with a huge grin, lumbered over and nudged his face close up to mine. "Do you know my brother? Do you know my brother? Do you know my brother Gerry? My brother?"

I stiffened, not knowing what to say to him.

"Alan, don't worry," Edna said decisively. "Maybe your brother will come another time." She took his hand and ushered him away from me.

Later I asked Edna about Alan. She only remembered his brother visiting once. So her use of the word "maybe" had been deliberate and profound. Not a promise, but a possibility. With her ability to size up a delicate situation, Edna had comforted Alan and rescued me.

Driving home that day, I decided that I would reach out to Alan's brother, if the village would give me his number. He had been sent an invitation, but maybe a personal phone call from another resident's sibling could help stir his interest. When I called, I told him I'd met Alan.

"I appreciate your calling," he said. "But I'm not interested. Don't get me wrong. I'm grateful Alan is at the village. But you have to understand. It's always been all about Alan."

"No, I do understand how that can be," I interjected, "but. . . ."

He began to get angry. "No, it's too much. I need to live my own life."

The conversation over, my first response was judgmental. How could he abandon his brother? But I also understood. I also wanted to live my own life. What I had failed to communicate, perhaps, was that the picnic could be part of the process. Then again, maybe not for Alan's brother. Another important lesson in learning that each person has to find his or her own way, and my way wasn't necessarily anyone else's.

And then there was another big surprise.

One Saturday after a particularly upsetting romantic disappointment, I decided to visit Edna. She was waiting in front of her house when I arrived.

"We have to go to the village food co-op to get eggs," she said, grabbing my arm.

When we pushed open the door, Edna called out, "Bill, come here now, Susan is here."

I saw a lanky, tousled haired young man bent over, taking cans out of a carton and stacking them on a shelf. Very slowly, he turned and straightened up, a can in each hand. Even at his straightest, Bill's shoulders were stooped, eyeglasses resting on a chain around his neck over a blue flannel shirt. But I could see that even though he was not making eye contact, he was good looking.

"Yeah, right," he said, continuing to stand there.

"I want you to meet Bill. He's my boyfriend."

"Yeah, right," he said again, without moving an inch.

"Bill, I'm Susan," I said, walking toward him, but careful not to get too close.

"Yeah, right," he repeated. "Edna is really nice," he said, looking down at the floor.

Like Bill, I was now staring at the floor, struggling to take in the reality of the words, "my boyfriend."

"We like to hold hands and sit next to each other at services and concerts," Edna explained later, when we were having tea in her house.

Edna had a boyfriend. They were innocent about sexuality, but steady in their feelings. This was a development that I had never foreseen.

I admired Edna. I envied her. I was happy for her. Yet, most importantly, I felt something uncoiling in me. Edna was on her own path. She was okay just the way she was, as perhaps I could be, too.

Chapter 15

Edna's life at Camphill relieved me of some of my burden of guilt that she would never lead a "normal" life. Even more, her way of being remained a touchstone for me as I set about trying to solve the complex puzzle of love and romance, and embarked on my second marriage.

I met Joel while having breakfast at the counter of a West Village coffee shop. Bearded, with ruddy cheeks, he exuded warmth as he offered to pour cream in my coffee. Would I like to model for him? he asked a moment later, explaining that he was a representational sculptor. "Just your foot. I'm just finishing a sculpture for a show I'm having in Brooklyn. I really mean that," he added, noticing me blush. And he did.

Within six months, I had moved into his fourth floor walkup apartment in the up-and-coming neighborhood of Park Slope. Baskets of red geranium blossoms and succulent jade plants thrived in our sunny kitchen window.

Joel was like a big teddy bear, and I loved the way he folded me into his arms. He had met my parents at the opening of his one-man show. They not only responded to his warmth, but also bought a small sculpture of a reclining woman.

"It will be beautiful on the landing of our staircase," my mother exclaimed.

One year later, when I was twenty-eight, our simple but elegant wedding took place in the brownstone gallery in Park Slope where his one-man show had been held. The gallery owners created a garland of flowers around an archway leading to the main room. The intimate group of about forty people cheered when Joel smashed the glass.

Edna sat next to me at our celebration dinner in a local Italian restaurant. Joel made sure to put his arm around her, too. I felt joyous. I was with a creative, loving man who would be a wonderful papa when the time was right.

As I moved into my thirties, my desire to be a mother became more intense. But I began to sense that although he had expressed an interest in children when we met, Joel was content to continue our life just as it was. That way he wouldn't have to worry about having to support a family. He had always lived a hand-to-mouth existence, selling a sculpture here and there, and as long as he got by, making art was central to his happiness. I sometimes pressed him about finding work.

"We want to adopt a child. I mean not now, but at some point, and we're going to need to be solvent," I said one night, as we were cuddling.

"I agree, but working more would take away from my studio time. And I need to feel you support my work as an artist. But I will try," he promised.

And he did make an effort to drum up commercial work that drew on his skills. I got excited when he got a commission to create bas reliefs for a company that made medals, but that prospect faded after he completed the first one. Little by little, I found myself paying for our life. I pressed him with how essential it was for him to make a better living. Children or not, I wasn't happy about supporting him.

But all his efforts to get jobs to supplement his meager income from art went nowhere.

Still, there was a brief moment when I was hopeful about our becoming parents. Through a good friend of his who had adopted children, we learned of a support group that helped prospective parents navigate the adoption process, and Joel agreed to go. Sitting next to him at an introductory meeting, I was aware of other couples conferring with each other and eagerly raising their hands to ask questions. These people were desperately seeking answers, as they grappled with the pros and cons of the many different avenues of adoption: foreign, domestic, private, or through an agency.

Obviously, becoming an adoptive parent was a major project that would require a solid commitment. But Joel wasn't asking any questions. It is so clear to me now that he had agreed to attend the meeting just to placate me. Perhaps if I could have gotten pregnant accidently, we would have found a way. But of course that couldn't happen. I felt a burst of raw, biting rage. Once again, my predicament seemed so unfair.

In my crystal ball, I saw myself as caretaker to a sweet but dependent teddy bear or the long-suffering wife of an artist. Neither of these roles was compatible with motherhood.

I glanced at the couple sitting across from me. I was in their camp. I, too, felt an irrepressible desire to find my baby. The possibility of adoption had been my fantasy solution to comfort myself as an adolescent. Perhaps when Joel and I met, it was still more of a vague idea. But now my longing was both palpable and, given the right circumstances, a realistic possibility.

I hit the shame wall and found it hard to fathom that I would be twice divorced by the time I turned thirty-two. Still, I had to face the truth. Though Joel had been a loving partner, marriage wasn't going to work for us in the long run.

When I confronted him about our differences, he didn't deny

anything. Nor did he try to fight for the relationship. Instead, he left me the apartment and moved out.

In this same period, Edna was experiencing her own troubles, which oddly paralleled mine.

She and Bill were still a couple. I invited them to spend a weekend with me at my new apartment in Manhattan.

"Bill, it's time to go, and bring your jacket," Edna reminded him, as we were getting ready to leave for the Botanical Gardens.

He readily agreed. Bill loved trains and was thrilled to be taking a subway ride. At the station, I bought him a map, which he studied all the way to Brooklyn. Edna and I smelled peonies in the garden, as he stood by. Except for the fact that Edna shared my bed and Bill slept on the couch, they behaved like an old married couple.

A few months later when I visited the village, in the midst of showing me a new garden, Edna stopped and said, "Bill and I would like to get married. We discussed it at a meeting with coworkers. We know we wouldn't have children, but we want to be married."

I went into slow motion. What a breathtaking idea. And how wise she was, with her awareness that having children was not right for her. A part of me was already dancing, but another was holding back. "Do Mom and Dad know yet?"

"No, I wanted to tell you first."

I asked if she wanted us to call them together.

"No," she said. "The village will speak to them when they visit next weekend." She had it all planned out.

But, alas, her dream of marrying Bill blew up in her face. When my parents phoned after their visit, they told me that the village refused to support the marriage. The door that had been so magnificently opened was now shut tight.

I didn't understand why the people who ran the village were so negative. The community was happy to recognize Bill and Edna as having a special friendship, but nothing beyond that. As I later learned, rather than being based on a spiritual or philosophical belief, the no-sex policy was a cultural attitude that harkened back to the turn of the 20th century, when Rudolf Steiner developed his framework called Anthroposophy, on which the village was founded. Steiner's thinking, a stew of Eastern and Western thought, embraced both Christianity and reincarnation. He wrote volumes on everything from an "etheric" level of existence to biodynamic farming. But I doubt if he ever made explicit reference to sexuality among the developmentally challenged.

I was furious. This was hypocrisy. How could the village be so egalitarian and then draw this line? A colleague of mine who worked with developmentally disabled adults told me that in her agency they actually counseled couples and helped them with sexuality. The outside world was changing in its attitudes, but not the village.

My parents and I had a long conversation. To their eternal credit, they had been open to the marriage idea. They even would have given permission for Edna to have a tubal ligation so she wouldn't get pregnant. That's how far they would have gone to give their daughter this happiness.

"Camphill is still the best solution, overall," my father said.

"It's not perfect, but we have to live with it," my mother echoed.

And over the years that became their mantra when other difficult issues arose.

I reluctantly agreed with them. It was true that Camphill offered so much compared to other programs. Still, the community's refusal to let my sister live fully as a woman hurt like crazy.

As I reflect back, there are other conversations I wish I'd had with Edna and my parents.

It still stings to remember her and Bill walking hand in hand. I wonder why I didn't try harder at the time to ask her how she felt. Yet, she wasn't one to express feelings, and I probably couldn't stand to explore something that had no solution. What's more, Edna seemed to take the decision in stride, though it couldn't have been easy for her. She rarely asked for things for herself, and the one time she did, it was denied. For some time she and Bill continued to behave as a couple. But over the years I noticed that they were together less frequently, and after a while the relationship seemed to wane. Occasionally, I would ask her if she had seen Bill.

She would usually reply, "Not too much."

When I asked her why, she answered, "He should have come to sit with me in the Hall, but he didn't."

About my parents: I wish I could tell them now how open-minded and compassionate I thought they were. I'd ask them how they felt about Edna having a tubal ligation, which would have shut the door on a bloodline grandchild. The painful irony of the situation! I would also have shared my fantasy of Edna giving birth to a child that I would adopt. A fantasy I knew was unrealistic, but which now could never happen. But at the time, none of us had the presence of mind or capacity for such conversations.

And though Edna was denied a marriage, she continued to embrace Camphill as her home. She contributed her special recipe for cheesecake to a village cookbook. She helped to lead the Sunday services, and she made a best friend named Susan. Among the diverse population of villagers, Susan was at Edna's level in her ability to read and write, and she even began to help Edna to write more legibly on lined stationery. This friendship was a stunning milestone for a girl who had few friends her own age. Edna's steadiness and fortitude became my model and helped me to move forward in spite of my own nagging doubts about ever finding a satisfying relationship.

❀

One of the most meaningful ways our lives intersected during that period took place at Carnegie Hall.

It was a fundraising event for the village, masterminded by parents in touch with world-class musicians. But the audience on that particular night wasn't there for the professionals.

Seated between my parents, I grasped each of their hands as one by one the members of the Village Ensemble made their way across the stage for their long-awaited performance. Suddenly, there was Edna, carrying her lyre and taking the last seat on the left in the first row. Susan, with her lyre, sat down next to Edna. Each of the thirty other villagers held a bell that played one note of the scale. Finally, Hannah, the inspiring coworker who led the group, walked across the stage and stood at the conductor's podium. She lifted her baton and very slowly the bells and lyres began to sound. Note by note, a Mozart melody. Nobody in the audience moved.

Edna, in her white blouse and the long navy blue skirt I had given her, was bent over her instrument. I felt as if I were spinning backward on a turntable, or in an Alice in Wonderland scene in which everything happened in reverse. Edna was on stage at Carnegie Hall, and I was in the audience. An alternate reality. I was stunned to see her so capable and dignified, concentrating on her task on this grand stage in front of hundreds of people.

I felt so proud, yet jealous too. I would never get to do what she was doing.

I also knew not to judge my feelings, because a moment later I was filled with sadness. This was an old emotion, stirred by old questions. Who would Edna be, if she weren't handicapped? What would it have been like for me to grow up with a normal sister? Would she have been more successful than me? Would my life be even harder if she weren't handicapped? In that imagined reality, I felt secretly, guiltily glad she was disabled.

The Mozart ended to thunderous applause, followed by a folk song. Somewhere in the simple melodic line curving upward, my cluttered thoughts released and drained away. Edna was living her own wondrous life that had nothing to do with labels about being handicapped. She was just Edna, playing her lyre in Carnegie Hall. And I was just her sister, Susie, listening in the audience.

Chapter 16

Carnegie Hall represented a moment of awe, wholeness and acceptance. Edna and I were each fine, just exactly as we were. For the next few days, I felt as if I were floating. My parents and I agreed once again that finding Camphill was a miracle.

"Edna was always musical, and now she's found a way to express it," my mother said.

"Camphill is on a solid footing. I think she will always live there" my father said.

Feeling freer to dream about starting my own family, I fantasized pulling a toddler on a sled up a snow-covered hill, and later reading *Good Night, Moon* to her. My favorite fantasy image involved walking around with a diaper bag on my shoulder and a baby in a back carrier.

But in the ongoing rush of life, the Carnegie Hall moment receded, and I fell back into my story of feeling hopeless about achieving my goal of motherhood. I also felt stagnant in my professional life: I was on my third agency job helping geriatric patients at a community health center, and working as a therapist two evenings a week in a mental health clinic. But without being able to pinpoint the source of my dissatisfaction, I sensed I was missing a comprehensive framework to support me as I tried to help untangle the myriad ways in which people were suffering. I also didn't yet have a way to make the leap from agency work to private practice.

Then I discovered psychoanalysis. In my mid-thirties, I became one of the first social workers to be accepted at The American Institute for Psychoanalysis, a prestigious institute founded by Karen Horney. At first I thought of analytic training as a steppingstone to opening a private practice, but my own analysis, a program requirement, became life changing in a far more personal way. Dr. Kelman, a wise and gifted man, could hold the depth and breadth of my experience. In my five years of treatment, we built a solid relationship in which I was able to revisit all the traumas in my life and find a new relationship to them. I had the luxury of time to slow down, speak, and be heard. Most importantly I had time to listen to myself.

Two years after starting at the institute, my private practice in the village was blossoming with referrals from my supervisors. I was appreciated for my sensitivity and intuitive way of working. But most of my own sessions continued to revolve around my romantic life.

When I was thirty-seven, I met Lenny. He was thirty-nine and had never been married or lived with anyone long-term. Still, he was emphatic about wanting a committed relationship. And though having children was not on his bucket list, he wasn't explicitly against it. What's more, I was encouraged by his willingness to visit Edna, and we spent a day with her at Camphill. As she showed us around, Lenny took special pains to draw her out by asking her questions about how the different crafts were made.

Dr. Kelman never gave me direct advice. Instead, he encouraged me to hold my conflicts in a compassionate way.

"If you keep allowing all your feelings and thoughts, the solution will be there," he would say.

And eventually it was, though not in the way either of us could have predicted.

Lenny was an oddball intellectual with a generous heart. He

was good at working with his hands. Savvy about real estate, he bought two lofts in the transitional Union Square neighborhood. To make money, he installed special lighting in hotels and restaurants, and bought odd lots of merchandise, which he auctioned off. One of his lofts was filled from floor to ceiling with assorted goods, such as fabrics, tiles, and bathroom fixtures. Lenny's gang of friends was family to him. And since many of them lived on the edge financially, Lenny thought nothing of giving them money or having them stay with him.

Growing up with Edna, I had learned to always see the potential in her; Lenny's combination of positive qualities inspired me to do the same with him. However, though this trait is essential for a sister or a therapist, it became a trip wire in my relationship with Lenny. I fantasized that his generosity in treating his friends as family would allow us to create our own family by having a baby. In my mind, being good with his hands meant Lenny could become equally adept at building cradles and toys. And a loft could become a home.

Yet, lying on the analytic couch, I couldn't keep lying to myself. After being together almost two years, I realized that, once again, I had been willing to suspend my clarity about what was important to me. Lenny had serious issues that could preclude commitment. The huge hot tub that took up half the loft living area when I met him remained uninstalled. We never stayed at his place because his bathroom was always going to be finished "next month." And the back area that he had once mentioned as a possible baby's room, remained piled from floor to ceiling with crates of widgets. Previously, I had tossed all of this into the "he's creative and a little bit of an eccentric" category. Now it looked like a flashing red warning light. Lenny may have given me a food processor for my birthday, but that didn't mean he wanted to set up a home with me.

I had to face this.

"I love being with you," he said, in answer to my question about where he stood on commitment.

"This can't go on," I said. "Something has to change. I'd like us to see a couples therapist."

To my surprise he agreed. I scheduled a couples therapy session, and felt hopeful again. But in a plot twist so bizarre it couldn't be made up, a dinner with his mother, who had flown up from Florida, became a game changer that made any future couples therapy session irrelevant.

For this all-important meeting, I tried to imagine how a future daughter-in-law should look and decided on sophisticated and sexy, but not too sexy. Wearing tight jeans and a soft blue cashmere V-neck sweater, I entered the Japanese restaurant. Lenny was already seated, his arm around a short woman with curly dyed red hair and dangling gold earrings. Neither of them got up.

"I'm very pleased to meet you," I said, in my warmest voice, holding out my hand to her.

"Oh, I always love to meet Lenny's girlfriends," Gladys said, shaking my hand, while winking at me.

I felt my stomach contract. Girlfriends, plural? As a therapist, I diagnosed her in my mind: possessive mother, threatened by me already. She clearly needed me to know how important she was to her son. I was one of many, but maybe, she feared, I was 'the one" who would displace her. Hence her need to trivialize me.

"I had to come up here, or it never would have happened. I always have to chase you down," she said to Lenny, jabbing him in the rib.

"This way you get to be in the jet set," he shot back at her.

Gladys was seductive and controlling, but with his wit, Lenny held his own.

I needed to stay grounded. I touched Lenny's arm and he flashed me a smile. Then he ordered sushi for the three of us to share.

"So you're a therapist," Lenny's mother said. "You may be able to give me some advice."

I felt flattered and eager to help, as the server set a huge platter of brightly colored sushi on the table.

"Lenny tells me you have a sister who is disabled, and she lives in a special community."

"Yes I do," I said, surprised and caught off guard. I usually reserved the subject of Edna for people I knew well. It was hard to imagine why Lenny would have told his mother about my sister. Feeling vulnerable, I tried to catch his eye, but his face was turning as red as the tuna.

"What kind of a place is this?"

I stumbled through telling Gladys that it was a life-sharing community, based on Rudolf Steiner's philosophy. She looked at me blankly. "It's a place where people who are so-called normal choose to live their lives with handicapped people," I continued, but before I had a chance to finish the sentence, she interrupted me.

"Does the state run this?"

I explained that though the village did receive some state funding, it was mostly self- sustaining.

"Do your parents pay for this?"

I had no idea where she was headed, but her tone felt oppressive, like a truck bearing down on me. I explained that Edna's Social Security was our contribution.

I kept trying to catch Lenny's eye and put my hand on his leg under the table, but he didn't reciprocate.

"I'd like to speak with your parents," his mother kept on.

"Mom, this is not the place," Lenny finally tried to interject.

I lifted up my chopsticks and carefully picked up a piece of salmon with bright red roe on the rice, as Gladys barreled on.

"Didn't Lenny tell you? I'm concerned about where my money is going to go after I die. I want Lenny to get it all. I thought your parents might be able to tell me how they are handling your inheritance, since you have this disabled sister."

I turned my hands upward in a gesture of incomprehension, as my eyes looked from her to Lenny.

"Didn't Lenny tell you that I had a son with Down syndrome, and that he was institutionalized?"

I turned to Lenny, now stuffing a piece of rainbow roll in his mouth.

"What is she saying? You told me you were an only child."

He put the chopsticks down, shrugged his shoulders and cleared his throat, but nothing came out.

"You have a brother, and you never told me he's in an institution?"

"Mom, I told you not to bring this up." Lenny was pleading with her to stop.

"Where is he?" I said, looking straight at her.

"Somewhere upstate," she shrugged.

"You mean, you don't even go to see him?" I persisted, looking from one to the other.

Gladys mumbled something about how her husband used to visit when he was alive.

"You spent a whole day with me visiting Edna, and you kept the lie going, even after that?"

There was a long moment of silence. "I'd even go with you to see him," I said to Lenny, reaching for his arm.

"I was young when this happened, so actually I have been an only child," he mumbled. It was as if a spring inside me had suddenly released and begun to uncoil. Lenny was holding up a mirror of my feelings, magnified a thousand percent. He was carrying the shame of a family, so intense that a child had to be hidden away. His guilt was so strong that he had to deny it. He hadn't just lied to me but was actually living his lie. I could see how he was tethered to a ghost that would always haunt him. His loft would never be cleared. Edna had just released me from an untenable relationship that might have dragged on for many more months, even years.

I was so lucky. Our family had found a way to stay together, even though we lived apart. Edna and I were present in each other's lives. It could be unwieldy. She had suffered in ways that were out of my control, and I still sometimes felt responsible. But we loved each other.

"Lenny and I broke up," I told her, when I called to say I was coming.

"Why?" she asked.

"He has a handicapped brother in an institution he never sees."

"Ugh," she said. "Some cows have had calves, and we can go visit them in the barn."

"I can't wait to meet them," I said.

Chapter 17

VERY SOON AFTER I broke up with Lenny, I had a pivotal dream that I brought to my session with Dr. Kelman.

At exactly 7:45 a.m., Dr. Kelman opened the door wearing his usual wrinkled jacket and expectant smile. Slipping off my shoes and rustling around to find a good place for my head, I lay down on the hard brown leather couch, pulled my knees up to my chest and put my arms around them. I could sense Dr. Kelman behind me. He had stubby legs which he usually crossed and uncrossed as he silently waited for me to begin. That was part of the opening ritual, which I always found comforting. He didn't disappoint today.

"This dream I had felt awful, although it was pretty simple," I began.

He remained silent.

"I walked down a street that turned into a dead end, and then I walked down another and another, and they all kept turning into dead ends, and that's the dream." I straightened my knees out and said nothing for a while.

"I know I'm depressed about the end of my relationship with Lenny and not feeling too hopeful about my life at the moment," I continued. "And I still feel that I'm to blame, that somehow I should have known better than to get involved with him."

"So this relationship was just another dead end," Dr. Kelman reflected back.

I could feel the tears welling up. I reached for the box of tissues set on a little table next to the couch. "This one was really hard to let go of without feeling I was too needy or that there will never be another."

We were both quiet. I could hear Dr. Kelman crossing and uncrossing his legs.

"Any other associations to dead ends?" he asked gently.

I paused, feeling a giant wave of sadness. "I can barely speak of it. Even now, I still hurt about how not fair it was that Edna couldn't marry Bill." I had told him before, but now it surfaced again, even though my parents and I still felt that the village was the best overall solution for Edna.

"The best solution, but still a kind of a dead end?" Dr. Kelman said, his voice tender.

Now I was overcome with grief for my sister. "Oh, Edna, you didn't get to do it." I reached for another tissue and said nothing for a long while. And then: "I still wonder if I'm holding myself back from finding a good relationship out of guilt and sorrow about Edna. I used to tamp down my excitement about the activities I did that she could never do. I can still see her and Bill holding hands, so hopeful and innocent. My personal brand of survivor guilt."

Another teary silence.

"I thought I had dropped the fantasy that Edna would give birth to a child, and I would adopt and raise it. But I'm having a new way to understand it now. It's less about passing on the family genes and more about how she would get to be part of something. Like together, we would be one whole person."

"That is something that may get clearer as we continue working," Dr. Kelman answered in his reassuring way. No guarantees, but a kind of calmness and perspective that he communicated, with the sense that we had time to work on it. That was the beauty and luxury of analysis. There was time to view the same issues in different contexts, and it was fine to keep bringing them up.

All of a sudden I had another thought. "Speaking of genes, my father, the world's greatest pessimist, once told me that since our family had come from a small Jewish community in Germany, perhaps there had been a lot of intermarriage. Between Edna and me, perhaps this was nature's way of ending the line. How could he say that? Even at that time I was so angry"

"He framed your family's life as a dead end. Perhaps that also fits with the Holocaust."

"Jesus, yes. Final Solution. He couldn't help himself; it was so ingrained in him. And in me too."

The phrase "end of the line" flashed through my mind again. "Oh my god, I see it. In the dream, it's not just that I think my life is going nowhere; it's that I myself am a dead end. The dead end is my body. I don't go anywhere. I just stop. I pushed the tube in till it hurt and couldn't move. Men's penises push in till they stop. They can't go all the way. Nothing can go all the way in. I don't go anywhere. The semen can't get through."

Sobs arose from the deepest place inside me. I was right there now, in my vagina, in the place where I couldn't go any farther. I had never gone so deeply into my sadness.

"Such grief, all the way in there." Dr. Kelman's voice was warm and comforting.

I sat up and turned to him. "I can't lie down, I need to see you."

He nodded and smiled.

"No children can grow there," I continued.

"That fact is true," he said. "And it is a great loss. You would have wanted that."

"Oh, you don't know how much."

He nodded again, "Maybe not, but I'm hearing the pain now in you. You have been holding it there for such a long time."

At last someone was hearing my sorrow.

"There are facts that we can't change, but we can learn to grieve our losses and continue our journey." Then he chuckled. "But enough of my lecture."

"No, you weren't that bad today. You're just doing that wise analyst thing."

"Well, in that case," he said with a big round laugh, "here's one more thing. When you were sixteen, you pushed a tube into yourself every single day. And as you've told me, it hurt. But there was no drama or fuss, you just went straight ahead and kept going. So really, you made yourself into the woman that you are. You created yourself, and you made it possible to be sexual and experience great passion. I know of no one else who has done anything like this. It took great courage. Look what you did with the facts."

I felt the silence of an opening, a way to hold everything, a connecting back and a trickling through. Dr. Kelman was saying that I could see all my hard work as an incredible accomplishment and part of the process of becoming the woman I was now. Nobody had ever said anything like that to me. Very deeply, I was understanding something huge about transformation. It was like a kaleidoscope that has the same number and kind of stones in it. We can't change the actual facts of our lives. Yet, with a flick of the wrist, we turn it ever so slightly, and the pattern rearranges itself and creates something new.

Chapter 18

I WAS ABOUT TO turn thirty-nine, and there was no man on the horizon. I could have been seriously depressed, but since the dream session, I had felt more confident. And when a new direction for motherhood presented itself, I was open to it.

The first step was to try my new idea out on my parents.

In between bites of sandwich over lunch at their house, I began by updating them on my many patients, as well as my reduced expenses, now that my analytic training was complete. My father told me how proud of me he was for having finished the program, and left to water the garden. I decided to break the news to my mother and leaned across the table.

"There's something very exciting I want to tell you." I paused and slowly exhaled. "I'm considering adopting a child on my own. I know it's not conventional, but it is very doable." I was talking fast and not really looking at her, as I laid out my plan to attend a support group called Single Mothers by Choice. I mentioned that the group was started by a single social worker, a friend of a friend, who was now the proud mother of a three-year-old.

I looked up to see my mother sitting with her arms tightly crossed.

"Mom you're not saying anything."

She peered intently at me. "You want to be a mother. It's a lot of work. I don't think you know what a hard job it is. And alone?"

I could feel my body contracting. "Yes. It's hard work, but I have a lot going for me. I'm in a profession where I can make my own hours. I can cancel when the baby is sick. I've saved money for childcare. And I have many close friends who support me. I think it could work."

"Susan, it's not the money. Look, I just don't think it would be a good idea for you to be a mother."

"What are you talking about?" My fingers curled into fists.

"You're very involved with your own things and you work in a demanding career," she went on. "Yes, I know you don't like to hear it, but you have a tendency to be self-centered, and. . . ."

At first I couldn't speak. I was stunned. My mother's response was so unexpected, so much more damning than I'd believed possible.

"I can't believe you're saying this stuff!" I yelled. "That's just great. I don't have a uterus. I can't have my own children, and now I don't even have a mother who will support my adopting one. This is a nightmare."

She pursed her lips and we sat in silence.

The great thing was that I didn't collapse. This wasn't about me, and I didn't have to take it in.

This was about how Eva hadn't been mothered during her own childhood. In her unexamined psyche, she believed I wouldn't make a good mother, because I hadn't been a good mother to her. Somehow, I was supposed to have made up for all the mothering she'd never received from her own self-involved mother. She had named me after her German governess, Susi, the only person who'd loved and cared for her.

And, of course, Eva had suffered from being Edna's mother. She must have been so frustrated and depleted at times. And she'd had to deal with my issues, too. No question, she had endured many painful experiences as a mother.

Yet, I had also been a mother to Edna, doing everything from buttoning her coat to teaching her how to float in the water. I had cut her meat, put on her gloves, held her hand crossing the street, helped decorate her room in the village, picked her up at Port Authority, and listened to my parents when they had been upset about her lack of progress. I, too, had suffered, learning to accept my sister's limitations while also experiencing joy at her accomplishments.

Sitting across from my mother, I wasn't fully confident that I could ever actually find my way to a baby. The jury was out on that. Still, as I tried to separate myself from my mother's cruel pronouncement, it became clear to me that if I was ever lucky enough to adopt a baby, I *would* know how to nurture and care for her.

I was going to the meeting.

Sliding into an empty rocker among five other women, I picked up the brochure on the coffee table and read, "While many of us would prefer a family with two loving parents, single-parent families can create stable, loving homes for children."

That was already sounding like second best. I glanced at the other women. Therapist or editor, I thought, looking at the woman to my left, noting her loose, flowing pants and long silver earrings. On the couch, two women, one with a grey streaked bun and wearing tiny gold hoops, and the other with short spiky brown hair, were probably a lesbian couple. The last woman appeared very young, probably in her twenties, and was wearing a jeans jacket over a flowered dress. The facilitator, a woman about my age, was seated near the coffee table. Her salt-and-pepper hair fell in soft waves, and she had on dark red lipstick.

Settling into the leader's chair, she clarified that she was a fellow traveler and not acting as a therapist for these meetings. Three years ago, she recalled, she had made the difficult decision to become pregnant through artificial insemination, and was now the mother of a wonderful son. She was here to help us share stories and learn from one another. I liked that she looked kind of sexy, as if she hadn't given up on finding a romantic partner.

As we went around the room introducing ourselves, the woman to my left revealed that, yes, she was a therapist.

"I haven't been in a long-term relationship," she said, "but why should I deprive myself of being a parent? My biological clock is ticking, so I already have an appointment for artificial insemination. This meeting is a reality check to make sure this is right for me."

The two women on the couch were indeed partners. One wanted a child and the other was ambivalent. The youngest looking woman hoped to adopt a baby, a calling that felt more important to her than having her own biological child.

I was next. "I'm divorced and haven't met anyone who would be right for me. I seem to meet all the men in New York who either already have children or who can't commit." People were smiling and nodding. "I will adopt, because I can't give birth. But I'm not sure I can give up the dream of having a partner." I stopped and sensed the silent support of everyone in the room.

Jane, the facilitator said she had gone through that too. She suggested that we consider some of the practical issues involved in being a single parent.

She passed around a checklist that covered finances, emotional support, childcare, and intimate relationships after motherhood. I felt quivery imagining coming home from work to a baby but no husband. And how would I feel waking up on Saturday morning and taking the stroller out by myself for a bagel and cream cheese? Hiring a babysitter so I could go out with friends at night would be fine. But coming home to a sleeping baby was no substitute for a partner to snuggle with. My parents would come around once there was a real baby. But in their seventies and living in Queens, how much babysitting could they really do?

And Edna. I could imagine her sitting in a rocking chair, singing as she rocked my baby. But in a practical way, she couldn't help.

Leaving the meeting, I felt confused but empowered. I had taken a step, even if I wasn't certain about single motherhood. Still, walking down the subway stairs, I suddenly felt empty. Instead of an adventure, single motherhood seemed more like giving up. I couldn't shake the thought that I really wanted a man to share parenthood with. But why? Not sure I had enough to give on my own? Afraid of loneliness? Maybe, but there was something else. I was already Edna's legal standby guardian, and when my parents died, she would be my sole responsibility. Adding single parenthood felt like too much soldiering on alone. But that still wasn't it.

The truth was that, although I had left two marriages, there were so many aspects of building a life with someone that I loved: creating a home, sharing mundane tasks, taking adventurous vacations. Besides, I had worked so hard to become self-aware. I was certain I would know when I found the right partner.

I felt a bit lighter. It was okay to still want this. And because of my anatomy, I had time. I didn't want to be an elderly mother, but I also didn't have the pressure of a ticking biological clock. I had a grace period in which to pursue adoption. What an advantage my anatomy was offering me. Another turn of the kaleidoscope! My hunched shoulders loosened. The option of single motherhood could always be revisited. I was so glad I'd gone to the meeting, but I didn't have to go that way. I had at least another couple of years to find a father for my baby.

Chapter 19

While I was inching my way toward motherhood, Edna had made a significant change in her life. She was now working outside the village three days a week at a local sheltered workshop that employed people with developmental disabilities. She'd gotten the idea after helping to show a group from the workshop around the village. During the tour, she'd met several people who were like her, only they lived at home and spent their days doing various jobs at the workshop.

In a phone conversation, I asked her how she'd managed to make this happen.

"I told the village care group that Bill was already volunteering at the local supermarket, helping to stock shelves," she explained. "Why couldn't I do something like that outside the village?"

The village coworkers agreed to the idea. Now, each morning Edna made her own lunch and waited for the bus to take her to work, where she stuffed lipsticks into boxes.

It was ironic that a sheltered workshop was the fate my parents had hoped Edna would escape when she went to Camphill. But in this context, the workshop was a path to greater independence and a larger life. There were supervisors, snack time, new routines, and friends. Her new friend Linda had even visited her in the village on a Saturday, and stayed for supper and Bible evening.

Edna's ability to advocate for herself and create opportunities in her seemingly limited life was an inspiration to me. What's more, viewing the workshop experience through her eyes, I learned to ease up on my judgments and let go of my tendency to label situations negatively. Watching what Edna did with the facts of her life offered yet another flick of the kaleidoscope. And though not a linear example of cause and effect, her way of seeing things helped me make my next major decision.

In early September, a couple of months after the Single Mothers by Choice meeting, I was milling around a party in a crowded, cavernous, smoke-filled loft near Gramercy Park. Finishing my second plastic glass of white wine, I felt a tap on my shoulder and turned toward a young man. There was something adorable about him. Maybe it was his dark curly hair or the baggy corduroy pants.

"Have we met?" I asked, looking into his inquisitive but friendly brown eyes.

"Not formally," he replied, "but I do know you."

"I'm sorry," I said, "but I've never seen you before."

"Well, I've certainly seen you. Give yourself some time, really think."

I could tell he was enjoying this, but I was starting to feel annoyed. "I haven't the faintest idea."

He explained that he was temping at my institute and had even typed some of my case reports.

I had a vague memory of a guy hunched over a typewriter. "You wear Birkenstocks."

"Yup," he said, pointing to his feet.

"I'm such a space case, I'm really sorry," I apologized, deciding I must be a snob not to notice the people around me.

"That's okay. You have beautiful eyes."

He was coming on to me. So young looking, twenty-seven at most, but cute. And I loved his biblical name: Seth. I hadn't been with anyone in a while, but he wasn't appropriate. I told him I was just leaving.

"I was thinking the same thing," he said quickly. "Maybe we could just take a walk."

I hesitated, but then we threaded our way out the door and down an elevator and began walking downtown.

He asked me about seeing a movie sometime.

"Really, that's sweet, but I don't know. I'm older than you."

"That's fine with me," he said.

"No, I think I'm a *lot* older than you."

"It's fine," he said, earnestly.

He had a lot of chutzpah to be asking me out. I was a trained therapist and he was a temp. Still, there was something appealing about his persistence. And he'd mentioned that he'd just applied to graduate school in psychology. We might have a lot in common. And it was a weird coincidence to have run into him at a party. Maybe he'd be good for a fling. Why was I so focused on meeting Mr. Right? There was plenty of time for that.

I wrote down my number.

When I got to the East Village movie theatre, Seth was leaning against a wall, his face buried in the *Village Voice*. I tapped him on the shoulder, and he smiled at me impishly. All through the latest Ingmar Bergman saga, his arm slung loosely around me, I felt both cozy and turned on. Afterward, sitting next to each other in a small, dark Indian restaurant, we swiped puffed bread in coconut sauce and fed each other.

Seth had worked as a film editor but was seriously considering graduate school in psychology. He had also written screenplays, including one about a young man who felt trapped by indecision over his career path. I felt drawn to the mix of his being lost yet self-aware, indecisive yet creative.

Spooning chutney over the chicken, I asked the inevitable question. "So, when was it that you graduated from college?"

"I'll be twenty-five in December."

Oh, god, no, I thought, even younger than I'd imagined. I told him that although he was younger than I'd guessed, I was probably older than he guessed.

"No kidding, so how old are you?" he asked, grazing his forehead with his forefinger.

"Thirty-nine, going on forty."

I watched him register surprise, then handle it by telling me I looked much younger than my age.

I thanked him. "But I'm not sure where that leaves us."

"Well, I just know I'm very attracted to you. Have been ever since I noticed your blue eyes at the clinic."

As he walked me home, I felt lost in my own indecisiveness. That he didn't seem at all fazed by my age was reassuring. But was this what I needed now?

When we got to my apartment house, we stood on the street for a few moments, and he touched my face with his hands. He looked so sleepy-warm and inviting, like something freshly baked from the oven.

When I think about the pressure I felt at that time to do right by myself, I can still feel the intensity of the conflict between my yearning for passionate connection and my search for a life partner who was interested in co-parenting with me. I didn't want to repeat history, but Seth was hard to resist. Now, I would want to tell my thirty-nine-year-old self: "Maybe you need to let go of some of that pressure, the tension of trying too hard to find The One. It's possible to keep your eyes open and still explore. Sometimes letting go can open things up in unexpected ways. You'll get what you want, though not quite in the way you imagined." But that part comes a bit later in the story.

The next Monday, after a patient cancelled, I wandered down the clinic hallway past offices with closed doors and others that were open, each with its own brown leather analyst's couch. Seth looked up and waved to me from the office where he was typing.

"You know, nobody ever uses that office," he said, motioning to the one across the hall.

My eyes followed his arm; then my body followed his. And there we were, door closed, holding each other on the analytic couch, stroking each other's hair, kissing hungrily.

"Always a good idea to mix the personal with the professional," I said.

"New use of analytic couch," he replied.

"Not too comfortable," I said.

"Not for daily use," he continued.

"No, maybe only three times a week, but not four," I said. Acting out sometimes is appropriate, I thought, edgy but okay, no real harm done.

"Whoops, patient coming in fifteen minutes. Gotta go."

The next minute I was out the door, hair pushed back, glasses on, holding my case notes, heading back down the hallway.

My faux pas on our next date highlighted my conflict between wanting a partner for passion and one who gave me a realistic shot at parenthood.

I had invited Seth over for my seduction dinner: chicken in a tarragon white wine cream sauce. Stirring cream into the wine, I fantasized us holding each other. I answered the downstairs buzzer, spoon still in my hand, and ran back to my bedroom to put on lipstick.

"This is scrumptious," Seth said, swirling the chicken in the sauce, placing a dripping piece of meat in his mouth. He leaned across the small table where we sat catty-corner, folded my hands in his, and pulled me toward him.

The next morning as we cuddled, he mentioned a football game on TV and said he was hoping we could watch together. I told him I knew nothing about football.

"Don't worry, I'll explain the basics. Beginnings are really important."

Beginnings are important, I thought, and this one feels so lovely. He began to draw a field with lines and numbers, adding arrows, labels, and writing down definitions of the different roles of the players. He asked me if it made sense.

"Kind of," I answered.

"Don't worry. It'll be clearer when we watch."

"You know, you would make a good father," I remarked, with no forethought. In the next second I bit my lip, disbelieving that I'd said that.

Seth stared at me, wrinkling his brow, for a few awkward moments.

"I don't know what made me say that," I said, back pedaling fast. "It's just that you're really patient and so good at explaining things, it just came out."

"No, it's okay. It's actually quite flattering."

"But we hardly know each other. It's nothing you should be concerned about."

"Well that's true, but it is flattering that you see me that way. And having a kid is something I'd like to do in my life at some point."

Right kind of person, wrong timing, I mused. It was good to experience what this was like. Using that as justification, I continued seeing him.

After three months of being together several times a week, I could no longer call Seth my fun fling. I was on the verge of falling in love. I initiated the conversation about the direction we were going. He said he had strong feelings for me but wasn't ready for monogamy. Sad but clear, I broke the relationship off. Luckily, that coincided with the end of his temp job at the institute.

Two months later he called. "I'd like to start seeing you again. I heard what you said about a monogamous relationship."

In a lengthy conversation, I told him I cared for him, but with our age difference, it felt crazy to contemplate a serious relationship.

"I agree with everything you're saying," he said. "But what I love about us is that even if we are a little crazy, we're both risk takers. I'd like to continue taking that risk."

I asked him again about being monogamous and again he said he was sure he wanted that.

I had to admit that his words had the ring of truth. If I could just get past my concerns about once again being outside the box of so-called normalcy because of our age difference, I could be with a man who was truly on my wavelength. A loving person who was there for me, and who, I was still sure, would make a good father.

Over the next few months, I kept finding magazine articles about older women dating younger men. Cher, at age forty, had moved in with a twenty-two-year-old bagel baker. Seth and I were now part of a trend. The articles stressed that older successful women didn't need their young lovers to have their lives figured out. Younger men were caring and open to new ways of working on relationships. That was my experience, too. But what would happen when I was fifty-four and

Seth was only forty? Would he still feel attracted to me? Even now, it was strange going out with his best friends. It was one thing being alone with him, but dinner with several other twenty-five-year-olds, no matter how accepting, made me feel old. I was in advanced analytic training and they'd recently left college. Some days I felt as if I couldn't do this. Why couldn't I just find someone my own age?

Yet, at other times, I felt a sense of trust in our deepening love. We visited Edna, who insisted on sitting next to Seth at lunch, after which he organized a game of catch with the villagers in her house. He was gentle and encouraging, and it felt natural to be there with him.

Seth had taught himself to use a Kaypro computer, one of the first PCs ever made, and then a bank hired him to do technical writing and teach others to use this new machine. He also continued to work on his own writing, while my private practice blossomed. He moved in, we had a Halloween party, put green Martian makeup all over our faces, and hung cobwebs everywhere. After everyone left, we kept dancing.

I was questioning our relationship less and less.

One Saturday morning we lingered in bed. "This is really serious," Seth said. "I have never loved anyone this way before." He told me he knew how important it was for me to start a family sooner rather than later.

And that was the morning we knew we wanted to get married.

I had waited and found the person who wanted to go the distance with me. Hopping out of bed, I ran to the phone to call my parents.

"Why do you have to marry him? Why can't you continue to enjoy living with him?" was my mother's response. She still didn't get it.

But I stayed calm. "And where would that get me, Mom? I don't need your approval. We're getting married, adopting a baby, and that's the way it is."

I wasn't surprised by her reaction. From the outside it might seem crazy to marry someone so much younger. But even though I was clear about how well we fit together, I could still write the old doom script from their point of view. *Our daughter keeps failing. This is her third marriage. He's unformed. And adoption is so risky. We know how hard it can be even having your own children. And yet another wedding?*

Of course there was going to be another wedding. Though my parents didn't understand, I was choosing to live more like Edna. I was taking the opportunity to trust my inner compass to create the life I'd wanted ever since a red-faced doctor had spoken those game-changing words to my vulnerable, sixteen-year-old self. That day a switch had clicked on with a message loop playing constantly in my mind: adoption, adoption. Mine was an unending longing to heal the trauma of that early wound.

Now there would be healing, and Edna would be part of it. For so long I had lived with the script of our handicaps. But the way was finally opening for me to transform the story; our family could now grow into the next generation. Edna would become an aunt. She would wheel the baby in a stroller all around the village, introducing him to everyone. And my parents would come around, because now there was a real possibility for them to become grandparents. Their own deeply buried hopes and wishes, concealed for so long in the darkness of dead ends, would be realized.

So, yes, there would be a wedding, even though my favorite aunt Hannah refused to come, saying two weddings had been enough.

It was held on an old barge tethered near the Brooklyn Bridge that was used for concerts but could be rented out for other events. With a fireplace, creaky wooden floors, an outside upper deck, and a view of the lower Manhattan skyline, the barge was the perfect setting for us and our hundred friends and family members. On a cold, clear Saturday evening in January, Seth and I said our vows under my first chuppah and before my third rabbi. Edna stood right beside me. After the ceremony, we sat at long wooden tables decorated with baskets of dried flowers and ate stuffed mushrooms and walnut pesto on homemade penne. My singer-songwriter friend, Roz, sang "I Will Survive," and another friend—a modern dancer named Rebecca—took to the floor with her husband, John, and did a dance in our honor. As the band began to play, I grabbed Edna and we swayed to the guitars, bass, and the rhythm of the tides.

Holding each other, Seth and I danced alone along the outside deck and, in the frosty air, clinked our glasses of champagne. Three was a charm. This was the one. Let the boat rock. I felt adored, deeply rooted, and giddy with joy.

Chapter 20

My mother never gave up trying to work things out between us.

A few months after the wedding, she floated an idea. She'd found a weekend workshop called "Mothers and Daughters" at the Omega Institute. It was to be run by two therapists who were, of course, mother and daughter.

"It's a chance to listen, to laugh and cry, and to heal old wounds," she said, reading the course description from the catalogue of New Age offerings. "I'd like to pay for us to go there."

When she said that, I felt myself grimace. It wasn't that I was surprised she was interested in Omega; she had always thought in unconventional ways. But with all the other differences in our family, growing up I hated that she went to yoga classes and Gestalt therapy and cooked Chinese food when everyone else was eating TV dinners. Why couldn't she just set her hair and play mahjong? Still, even as a child, I was also drawn to the mysterious way her mind worked, which led her to make choices such as Camphill. And when I was diagnosed, she'd found me a therapist at a time when most mothers wouldn't have even conceived of therapy for their teenage daughters. Most important, as difficult as she could be, my mother always wanted us to have a better relationship. So here was another one of her offbeat ideas. Part of me recoiled at this opportunity for intimacy and sharing. Would this turn into another instance of her saying she knew me better than I knew myself, or that I didn't make good decisions?

I couldn't remember a time when we had ever gone anywhere, just the two of us. It was scary to imagine. Luckily, we would be with other people within the structure of the workshop. And there was always the chance that we might connect in a better, more authentic way.

We opened the door to a musty cabin with camp beds and simple dressers. Late-afternoon light flooded in through the open door. I threw my bag on the floor and sat on a bed, watching the ritual of my mother unpacking and arranging everything. First, she placed her books on the night table. Then she checked to make sure the reading lamp worked and that the pillows and blankets were adequate. From there, she moved on to the closet to assess the hanger situation, and then, lastly, she took out the travel alarm clock. According to my mother's code, it was never good to rummage through a suitcase. You pack exactly what you need, and then you arrive at your destination and set up your life. This was so familiar. We'd done it many times as a family on trips.

Watching her, I found myself feeling both amused and touched. It occurred to me that my refugee mother had learned to travel light, unpack quickly, and get on with her life. This was how she'd learned to survive. I felt a burst of tenderness.

"Mom," I teased, "I knew I could count on you for the alarm clock."

"So, that's not so bad, is it? Your old mother can still think of these things."

"You're not that old. At seventy-six, you're pretty spry coming to a place like this," I said. I had already gotten something out of the workshop.

And though I didn't share that insight with her then, the next morning I did share with her the important discovery that she snored.

"It's sort of a soft whistle," I said, to her vehement denials. "And Mom," I added in my most mock-serious voice, "we came here to work on our trust issues. You can trust me on this." We both started laughing.

A short while later, we opened the door to a large, sun-filled room and found seats among the group of about sixty women. The two therapists stood up front, helping each other to pin on their microphones. Sally, obviously the mother of the pair, was a solidly built woman with gray curly hair. She wore dangly earrings and a long, flowing skirt. Her daughter, Tricia, with her diamond stud earrings and fitted corduroy slacks, conveyed a delicate but firm quality. Together, they described the workshop, which would start with easy exercises and move on to some that might elicit deep feelings. Using their own relationship as a model, I watched them disagree and interrupt each other in a friendly respectful way.

"Mom, it wasn't that way for me."

"Oops, right you are. Teaching moment. It is often my daughter's job to educate me," Sally said, laughing.

I found myself liking them both. They kept saying that a relationship was a work in progress, and they acknowledged both the gift and the struggle of their connection.

Our first exercise was to share a memory of a positive experience we'd had with each other. I thought of one of the few times my mother had comforted me. I was about seven. Waiting for the bus after school, I was part of a game that involved jumping over rows of school bags. I had to pee badly, but was holding it in. As I hopped over someone's pencil box, I lost control, and the pee came rolling down over the box. I ran out of the schoolyard and didn't stop until I made it up the four flights of stairs to our apartment. My memory was sitting in my mother's lap, crying.

Her memory was my performance of Captain Hook walking the plank in the camp water ballet. My aluminum foil hook had fallen in the water after I'd swaggered up to the edge of the diving board. I'd jumped off and seemed to disappear.

"You swam under the dock through muddy muck, and surfaced way to the side. I admired you so much," she said. She didn't often praise me that way. A feeling of warmth spread through me.

Next we shared something about ourselves that the other person didn't know. I told her about the swimming lessons on Long Island Sound when I was six. Unlike later during my star turn as Captain Hook, I was afraid to jump in the water and sat on the dock the whole time. When she picked me up, she asked why my bathing suit was so dry and I told her I'd jumped in, but my suit had dried in the heat.

"You became such a good swimmer anyway," she said.

"Mom, that's not the point. I lied to you because I wanted you to think I had it together. I was already trying to make up for Edna."

"I never wanted you to have that burden."

"You paid me to play with her."

"I know it was hard for you. And I appreciate what a good sister you've always been to her. I was probably too strict," she added.

"Well, you were strict, but I don't think you're getting the real issue that I couldn't really talk to you."

She told me she was listening, and that fit with what she wanted to tell me. When I was born, the prevailing philosophy was to feed babies only every four hours. She wanted to feed me when I cried, but she did what the doctor had told her. And even though my face got so red from crying, she ignored her natural impulses.

"Oh, Mom, you were listening to me. I always think of you as being so strong and independent, like leaving Germany on your own, or going back to college when Edna and I were little. But in this situation you just did what you were told, and I have done that so many times."

"We were both so miserable," she said sadly.

I reached over and took her hand in mine.

In the afternoon the exercises got more serious.

We were to think about something we didn't feel we had permission to do or be or feel. We could give permission to ourselves or ask the other for permission, and see how we felt after that. We were actually to get on our knees to ask for permission.

I got down on my knees, and took my mother's hand in mine, tears already washing over my face. She was looking at me intently. She knew what was coming, and I sensed her being open.

"Mom, I need permission to be a mother. I need it from you."

Now I was really crying. She nodded. I could see in her eyes that she'd heard me. She was finally getting how important this was to me.

She squeezed my hand. "Yes, of course I give you permission. I'm sorry for what I said. And I will help you. I will, in whatever way I can. I promise you."

We embraced.

She reached into her pocket and produced a packet of Kleenex. I took one and didn't even think about teasing her for being prepared.

She then told me about her older, very handsome cousin Robert and how in love with him she'd been. When he visited, he would always bring presents and spend time with her. But when she was fourteen he was killed in a train crash and she was devastated. Afterward, she stayed in her room crying, but that was the last time she had ever wept.

She was telling me something huge. It was true; I had never seen her cry. She hadn't cried since she was fourteen: not about leaving Germany, not about Edna, not about me, not about anything.

She moved her chair and knelt down in front of me. "I need permission to cry," she said.

"Oh, Mom, I give you so much permission to cry."

I took her face in my hands and gently removed her glasses. Her pale blue eyes were moist, and she was blinking. Something more was needed. My fingertips grazed the top of her short wiry hair, and my throat tightened. A frantic fear moment of too much closeness. I swallowed and closed my eyes, and gradually my hands began stroking her head. We had never shared such a vulnerable moment.

Chapter 21

FEELING THE FULL support of my parents and a year into our marriage, Seth and I got serious about adopting. Our first step was to attend a conference sponsored by a self-help group, Adoptive Parents Committee.

Pulling into a large parking lot at a college in Westchester, I felt strangely depressed. Seth turned off the motor, and I sat there, not moving. The closer we got to trying to adopt, the more impossible it seemed. I'd gone to meetings before, but inside I still felt hopeless.

"C'mon, this conference is going to be good," Seth said.

"I'm scared it won't help."

"It will be fine," he assured me, pulling the key out of the ignition and squeezing my hand.

Once inside the building, I noticed an earnest-looking couple in their forties. The man was kneeling in front of a toddler trying to unzip a jacket, while the woman, carrying a newborn in a Snugli, was bent over trying to help. Such a sweet tableau. Will I ever be figuring out those kinds of logistics? I wondered.

Seth steered me down a hallway thronged with men wearing expensive-looking suits, women in sweatpants, some with gray hair, others in their twenties, interracial couples, and two women with arms linked. A couple walked slowly past us shepherding a pigtailed little Down syndrome girl between them. I turned my gaze away. Way too hard for me to consider.

We stopped in front of a door taped with an oak tag sign: "Independent Adoption—Everything You Need to Know for Success."

"We've already decided to adopt independently and we know this stuff," I complained.

"Yeah, but there's going to be info about ethical attorneys, and we really need specifics on how to get started. Which is what we do want to do, right?" Seth led me into the room. Seated around the conference table, a woman with shoulder-length gray hair smiled at me, and I found myself smiling back.

The workshop facilitator, a thirty-something man with a neatly trimmed beard, cleared his throat and told us that the most important thing he could say was that anyone in the room who wanted to be a parent could be. "It can and will happen for you." He went on to explain how one of his two children came from the Pacific Northwest through an independent attorney, and the other from Asia through an agency. He explained that because the process could be rocky, it was important to repeat the mantra again and again: "It can and will happen for me."

This man understood how I felt. A slight thrill rippled through me, and with it came the vision of a diaper bag with a shoulder strap and lots of compartments. Maybe I should buy one to assure myself that *this can happen for me.*

I returned back to what the facilitator was saying, and the words *special needs children* whizzed by. I want a healthy infant, I thought. Is that too much to ask? If my child has issues that come up along the way, okay. But I can't start out that way. I'm already Edna's standby guardian. I could see the diaper bag floating away.

I glanced over at Seth, who was writing down the names of ethical attorneys in the tri-state area. It was important to work with someone who wasn't "buying babies on the black market." With independent adoptions, we would contact potential birth mothers through ads in newspapers. Then, if they responded, we would refer them to our attorney.

"Remember," the leader said, "you have to be persistent. Situations fall through, because birth mothers sometimes change their minds after the baby comes."

Situation was the euphemism for a pregnant woman seeking adoptive parents. He reiterated that we should continue on to the next *situation* if one fell through.

I was persistent like my survivor parents who kept going and going. But a voice inside still warned, "Don't kid yourself; you could do everything right, and it still might not happen for you."

"How do we pick states to look for situations?" I heard a woman ask.

"Women get pregnant everywhere," the facilitator replied.

It's a crapshoot, I translated to myself.

"I heard Texas was a good place to try," someone piped up.

"Possibly, but don't get fixed on any one place. A lot of babies are born in New Jersey, too."

I looked up and smiled, in spite of myself. Seth leaned over and whispered, "See? Babies are born everywhere. All we need is one."

Maybe I am entitled to my own crapshoot, said a voice inside me, as I got another glimpse of the diaper bag. This one had a light blue and white pattern, because blue could work for a boy or a girl.

Many ads by prospective parents said something like, "Let us help you in your time of need," but that seemed patronizing. I decided on, "Let's help each other." Seth and I installed a dedicated, unlisted phone line to preserve our anonymity, and so we would know when a potential birth mother called. I rehearsed our message over and over to sound as warm as possible: "Please don't hang up. Your call is so very important and valuable to us. We will return your call as soon as we possibly can and would love to speak with you." There were so many ads. Everything hinged on my voice.

Less than two weeks later, we received a message from a young woman who said she would call us back but left no number.

It was a miracle to get a call so soon. Many people waited for months. All week we rushed to the machine to check for another message the second we got home. And every time there was none, my heart sank. Twice the phone rang, but when I answered all I heard was a click. At the end of the second week, on a Tuesday night, the phone rang again.

"Hi, I left you a message a little while ago. I'm six months pregnant and I liked your ad," said a voice, sounding both upbeat and casual.

It was the same young woman who'd left the message. We spoke for an hour, Seth and I passing the phone back and forth. Her name was Brenda, and she lived only two hours out of the city. She'd been to an adoption agency, but had walked out because she wanted more control over this momentous decision. She wanted to be the one who chose the adoptive parents. I loved that about her. What had drawn her to us was my phrase about helping each other. We told her everything we could about our longing for a child, our loving relationship, and all the opportunities we could offer a child.

"You are the ones," she told us. "I'll be calling you again soon."

"That's beautiful," I said, my heart thumping like crazy. "When you're ready, you need to call our attorney."

"I'll take the number now," she replied.

It was only as I was falling asleep that night that I realized she hadn't asked anything about our ages.

From there a relationship began that seemed very promising. Brenda got in touch with the attorney and called us from time to time to report that she'd seen the doctor, and all was going well. She confided that she had been living in her car, but now her parents, who earlier had thrown her out, had decided she could live with them. I kept telling her how brave she was. At times, the workshop leader's voice echoed in my head: "Situations do fall through." There was no guarantee. We might not get this baby. Yet, Brenda was confiding so much in me that I dared to hope.

Three months later the call came.

"Hi," Brenda said. "It's a girl, and you could come to see her tomorrow."

I heard myself screaming to Seth, and felt my heart burst with love. *I have a baby and it's a girl, my most special wish!* All this time I'd imagined holding a little girl. I had not grown up among many boys and felt more comfortable with girls. But on a deeper level, mothering a healthy daughter was a way to repair my relationships to both my mother and my sister. And now she was here and we could go see her. Just like that. Done. I had leaped through the fire hoop of all those deafening *noes*, *dead ends*, and *not evers*. I'd succeeded in burning through whatever karma, emotional baggage, or psychic craziness had held me back.

"We did it," yelled Seth, running toward me, both of us screaming, "It's a girl," and twirling each other around the apartment. And as we danced, I reached for the diaper bag that hung over the closet door, and slung it around both of us.

Before this call came, I had held onto my skepticism. Even as we got closer and closer to adopting, I protected myself from disappointment with my negative thoughts. Today, though, I could sense another reality. A whole package of family pain and beliefs no longer had to be my truth. And the curse of my anatomy had just been superseded by the supreme truth that I was receiving the gift of all gifts, and that I would do everything in my lifetime to be worthy of it.

I dialed Edna.

"You are the aunt of a little girl," I cried.

"That's great," she said. "What's her name?"

"Rebecca, and you will see her soon."

"I'll tell my house parents at lunch, and then announce it at Bible evening on Saturday," Edna said.

Our joy was Brenda's sorrow.

On a cold, cloudy April morning, we borrowed Seth's parents' car and drove upstate. Map in my lap, my mind drifted. What would our baby daughter look like? Would she feel like mine? What if she didn't? I started to worry out loud.

"She will be our beautiful baby and we will love her," Seth said, patting my leg.

I reached for the plastic shopping bag and pulled out the red hat and flannel onesie patterned with teddy bears that we'd brought Rebecca to wear home. "I hope she'll like this," I said, giggling.

When we saw the sign for the hospital, my heart started beating faster. I was out of the car the second Seth pulled into a parking spot. At the Obstetrics Department, they already had our names. A smiling LPN led us into a lounge.

"We'll bring her to you," she said.

Not five minutes later, a nurse appeared, a wrapped bundle in her arms.

"Why don't you sit in the rocking chair," she suggested.

And there she was. Eyes closed, long lashes, and an adorable cowlick sticking straight up. I put my arms around her lightly, afraid to smother her, and began to rock.

"This is so good," the nurse said. "We're so glad you're here. We've been trying to pick her up and hold her as much as we can."

"Hi, honey," said Seth, taking a turn.

I had to have her back soon.

Holding her face next to mine, I nuzzled her head with my nose to smell her baby-ness. If I kept touching her, maybe I would believe she was mine. Her skin was so soft, warm, and downy. I couldn't get enough. I had to keep touching her, because it was impossible to take in that she was my baby. I hugged this sweet little being to let her know how much I loved her, and to feel her preciousness inside my body. My baby. My baby girl. The one who couldn't come through me, but came to me this way. Already, I was making up how I would tell her when she asked. "You grew in another lady's tummy, but you were coming to me. You just had to find another way."

That way began in a hospital, but there was no blood or screaming or shots or pain for me. Down the hall was the woman who had screamed and moaned and then phoned us when Rebecca was born. Brenda had decided not to hold her, so she wouldn't get attached. So strong, that woman.

And now for the part that would require the most strength: Brenda and Seth and I and a hospital administrator had to meet in a conference room to make the adoption final, while a nurse held Rebecca in another room.

A young woman with shoulder-length, dirty-blond hair stood up when she saw us. Brenda was shorter than I had imagined, with blue eyes and a sweet smile. I grabbed both her hands. Seth stood close. Then we all sat down, tears streaming down our faces. Brenda wanted to know what name we had chosen.

"Rebecca," I told her, "one of my favorite names from the Old Testament. Rebecca was both beautiful and compassionate, giving water to the camels at the well.

"I like that," Brenda said, looking away.

We asked if she had thought about what was next for her. She mentioned going to school to become an LPN. She couldn't have taken care of a baby now, not by herself, she added, and her parents had refused to help. But she was determined to change her life.

I wished I could help and comfort her, but it was time to sign the papers. This amazing woman was entrusting her baby to us and forever letting her go. We could never heal the sorrow of her loss. But we were entwined, and Brenda would always be part of our lives, even if we never saw each other face to face again.

I had never been religious, but was open to spirituality. Driving home, the Yiddish word *beshert* came to me. It commonly means *divinely meant to be*. This usually, but not always, refers to finding a soul mate or partner. But for us, it was finding our baby. And now here we were, having placed the ad in January, on our way home with Rebecca in April. It could have been the result of chance or dumb luck, but it didn't feel like that. It felt *beshert*. A miracle that for me was as great as the parting of the Red Sea.

Chapter 22

My parents were over the moon about being grandparents. For Rebecca's first birthday, they joyfully threw her a party. This was completely out of character for them. In my childhood, birthdays were subdued affairs with lovely presents and a cake, but no parties. There were no explicit reasons given, but I believe they were loath to give me a party when Edna had no friends and wouldn't be having one. It was easy to get around it, because my birthday is in summer and we were usually away. And because I don't remember going to many other children's parties, it didn't dawn on me until I was an adult that perhaps I had missed out. So, anticipating Rebecca's first birthday party felt very exciting.

Seth pulled the car into the driveway of my parents' new home. They'd recently moved to a care community for senior citizens in Rockland County based on the same principles as Camphill. Remarkably, Edna had been the channel to help my parents figure out how to live well as they aged. They had found Edna the village, and through Edna they'd discovered The Fellowship Community. Edna took care of us just by being who she was.

We opened the door to a living room filled with pink and white balloons. Rebecca screeched, and I struggled to get her jacket off as she went careening through the balloons. A little party was one thing, but I couldn't compute that my staid mother had created this colorful chaos. She beamed as she introduced me to her yoga teacher, their accountant, and new friends in the community. I watched my father smile as his eyes darted around the room trying to follow Rebecca's rapid trajectory. Later, as she bent over to put the cake with lit candles in front of her granddaughter, my mother's eyes were shining. More than just keeping her promise to support me, she was celebrating and loving this child. I realized once again that this healthy, lively little girl, the joyful center of our lives, had been a gift impossible for my parents to dare to imagine. But on that day, I was able to drink in the grand truth of us as a family having fun with pink balloons.

Yet reflecting on this moment now, it's painful to realize that Edna wasn't there. Even more difficult is realizing that the possibility wouldn't have even been broached. Woven into the wallpaper background of our lives, it was simply a given that there were times when Edna couldn't be with us. Logistically, getting her to and from my parents' home would have required a two-hour drive each way. What's more, her visits to my parents inevitably created tension, since they would have to rearrange their lives around what she enjoyed, like spending an hour at a five-and-dime store. For them, having her there would have interfered with their enjoyment of the party. At the time I, too, would have worried about whether she was bothering some of the guests, or hoped she was enjoying herself. It wouldn't be easy to tell.

But even in her absence, Edna was a presence. Somewhere in the space between the balloons, she was among us: the other daughter and the sister, the aunt, the one who didn't, the one who wasn't, the one who couldn't. It is only now that I miss her being there.

Thanksgiving week was always a time when Edna visited my parents. And on the Tuesday of Thanksgiving week when Rebecca was about two and a half, Edna called to report a big change in our mother.

"Mom gave me a sealed envelope and said it was an early Hanukkah present, but when I opened it there was nothing inside."

My father got on the phone. "Your mother is acting strange. She has the table set and insists today is the day. When I say Thanksgiving is Thursday and I need a shopping list, she says okay. But she hasn't made the list. I don't know what to do."

Two days later we had Thanksgiving dinner in a diner. My mother moved the food around her plate, but ate nothing. Mostly, she stared at us blankly. There was something radically wrong: depression, memory loss, confusion? Nothing I had any experience with. I tried to force down the fake mashed potatoes and hoped the doctor would diagnose what was wrong.

While this behavior seemed sudden, I understood later that my very intelligent mother had hidden signs of her oncoming dementia. I found written lists and reminders on her desk. There were other clues I might have picked up on, such as my always-prompt parents arriving late to visit us, or the long rambling speech Eva had made at Rebecca's baby naming. But as sometimes happens with dementia, when she slid, she slid fast.

My mother was on a downward spiral from congestive heart failure, as well as progressive dementia. Still, she and my dad were able to continue living together in their apartment in the community, which helped to care for her. And though she spent most of her time sitting in a chair not remembering things, sometimes she surprised us. One afternoon she got up, sat down at the piano, lifted her hands over the keys, and played a whole Bach two-part invention. Tears flowed from my father's eyes as he watched her.

"I had her back," he told me on the phone the next week. "But now she's returned to being the way she has been."

She never touched the piano again.

By the time Rebecca turned five, my mother was spending most of her time in bed. One spring afternoon I sat with her, holding her hands in mine, feeling shy and a little uneasy. Although we had grown closer, there had never been much physical affection between us. I noticed how much smaller she looked, no longer the imposing figure of my childhood. I rummaged through her favorite books: Martin Buber, the Kabbalah, and Edgar Cayce. She believed in reincarnation. I remembered how she used to tell me that, from a Kabbalistic point of view, there were places in the Bible that pointed to that belief.

That afternoon she picked up a book, read one sentence, and then put it back down.

I noticed a jar of her favorite hand cream on her tray and began rubbing the cool white salve between her graceful fingers, which could span an octave. They still felt surprisingly flexible and strong. I pushed up her pajama sleeves and began applying gentle strokes up her arm. She smiled and motioned to me that she wanted to sit up, so I rearranged her pillows.

"I wish I could help you. I know you are afraid of dying," she said, her pale blue eyes clear and alert.

I stopped rubbing. Out of nowhere, this lucid sentence entered the core of my being. How did she intuit this? I loved this moment, knowing her consciousness could shift in a flash.

"Why?" she asked.

"It's eternity," I answered. "That it lasts forever and ever scares me."

She was silent. I reached for her hands again and began to caress them.

"We go on in our relationship to God," she said. "We are part of this bigness." I kept stroking her hands. Something about her voice telling me this felt both awesome and comforting. It was about nearness, her nearness to me, her nearness to death, my nearness to her. The idea of being in a relationship to God, which is part of the mystery of eternity, felt profound. But that my mother was stepping into a moment of clarity was as close to being with God as I had ever been.

She lay back on the pillow and closed her eyes. We sat a while longer.

"A yellow jacket," she said, opening her eyes again. "In the basement."

"What do you mean, Mom?"

"It's in the basement," she repeated.

I had no clue what she meant. "Tell me. I want to know."

She looked at me a little blankly, but I sensed her struggling to express something. "Rebecca," she said, closing her eyes.

"Oh there's something for Rebecca in the basement. I'll look," I said, realizing she must mean some box with stuff she'd picked up at a yard sale. She had loved collecting toys and clothes for Rebecca that way.

When I turned on the light in the basement, I remembered Rebecca squealing with joy as she dipped her feet in a wading pool my mother had found for her. And when I opened the cardboard box at the foot of the stairs, a yellow rain slicker popped out at me. A little big, but something she could grow into.

I ran up the stairs and into my mother's room. "I found it," I called out. Then realized she'd fallen asleep.

"I found it," I repeated to myself. Nudging the door closed, I hugged the slicker to my chest and stood there sliding my hands up and down the smooth yellowness of it.

Two days later, my father called me early in the morning to say that my mother had died during the night. He also thought she had turned off her night lamp, something she hadn't done for months. To my mind, that had been my mother in a lucid moment knowing the end was near. It was as if she were taking charge, saying to herself and to us that it was time to turn off the light and turn toward her next phase. This detail, both practical and profound, was the one that started me sobbing.

Moving toward the end of her life, struggling through the fog and layers of memory loss, she had become the mother I always wanted. She comforted me about my deepest fears, offering solace that she'd been unable to give while I was growing up. And at the very end, in remembering the slicker, she affirmed my deepest dream of becoming a mother.

We had healed it all.

CHAPTER 23

EDNA TOOK MY mother's death in stride, having been made aware of her decline. In the village, as one nears death, the process is referred to as "approaching the threshold." Edna had witnessed several villager friends get sick and die. She'd adopted the belief in reincarnation and was prepared when Eva passed away.

"I will miss our mother," she told me as we sat together holding hands, waiting for the service to begin. "Me too," said Rebecca, sitting on my other side.

"What will you miss about Grandma?" Edna asked.

"How we went swimming in the pond, and when she would say *ja ja* in German," my daughter answered.

"That's nice," my sister said. "I remember how she gave us bubble baths, and Mommy and I were in the tub together."

I gave each of their hands a big squeeze.

Shortly after our mother died, Edna was taken to the local emergency room and admitted following a severe asthma attack, during which she almost died. She'd had asthma before, but until this point it seemed to have been managed with homeopathic remedies, which the village doctor favored.

Though our mother's death might have been one stress factor contributing to Edna's attack, it wasn't the only one. My sister felt unsupported by her current housemother, Rima. And since I'd gradually been taking on more responsibility for Edna's wellbeing, after the attack I needed to advocate for her in a way that was both proactive and skillful. I was convinced that some aspect of the asthma was her cry for help. Maybe she had gotten so sick because she didn't feel she could complain or say what she needed.

A couple of months before the attack, I asked Edna how she liked living with Rima.

In a rare expression of feeling, she answered, "Rima always pays more attention to Ally."

"Like how?"

"When Ally gets upset she takes her to the cafe, but when I need a haircut, she doesn't have time."

I, too, had experienced Rima as brusque and unapproachable, and wouldn't have wanted to live with her. I'd considered speaking with Rima then but had felt intimidated. It was the policy for the coworkers to decide where the villagers would live, without consulting their families. But after the asthma attack, I was determined to be a force to help Edna.

Driving up to see my sister, I decided to speak to Rima alone. I found her in the kitchen and asked if she had a moment to talk. She suggested tea.

Carrying a tray with cloth napkins, a pot of tea, mugs, and biscuits into a small study, she began, "Good that Edna is over this crisis."

I agreed that Edna had come through a rough moment. Then I mentioned that she'd told me there were things that were difficult for her in the house. "I thought you'd want to know that she sometimes feels a little left out."

"How is that?" Rima said, in a clipped, tight way.

I explained that although I realized Edna could be bossy, which could be off-putting, I also understood that when she was bossy it was because she needed nurturing.

"Edna told me you prefer Ally," I said next, throwing it all out on the table.

Rima acknowledged that. Yes, Ally needed a lot of attention. Then, cradling the tea mug in her hand, she added, "Well, you wouldn't want me to lie to you."

I felt her straining.

"I can't force myself to behave in a way that I don't feel. Edna is difficult for me."

I was seething and wanted to scream, All she needs is kindness and affection, which you don't seem to have a clue about, and it's led to an asthma attack!

But instead I went with, "I appreciate your honesty, but now you know how Edna feels. She's very aware." I flattened the tea bag with my spoon. "I know the coworkers look at many factors in deciding where villagers live, but maybe this house is not a good fit for Edna."

"It's a thought," Rima replied.

A few weeks later, with excitement in her voice, Edna called to tell me she was moving to a new house with house parents who had recently joined the village.

Zalene, Edna's new housemother, was the opposite of Rima. I sensed her eagerness to connect the moment I first spoke to her, when she invited us up to have a picnic at her house. With a warm clarity in her eyes, Zalene was American, in her late thirties, married, and mother to a boy and a girl close to Rebecca's age. Our visits became something we all looked forward to: Rebecca, because she was now old enough to run around the whole village with her two new friends and hang out in the barn with the pigs and cows; Seth, because he could go for a run and feel comfortable asking to use a shower on his return; and me, because Edna was healthy and thriving. I also noticed how Zalene was a model for Rebecca in accepting and enjoying Edna.

When Rebecca was a toddler, she would sit in Edna's lap for her to read a story. But as she got older, she began to keep more of a distance. Now I noticed her joining Edna in setting the table. And as a wonderful surprise, Zalene was becoming a friend with whom I could really talk, a pleasure that never would have happened with the generally reserved European coworkers.

"Edna's so helpful, she knows all the rituals, what candles to put where, and that's so good, since I'm not familiar with all these things," Zalene told me as I helped her make lunch. We had discovered that we both liked trying new recipes, and I had brought all the ingredients for a warm spinach salad: olives, feta cheese, spinach, mint, and olive oil.

"I'm so glad you appreciate her," I offered. "Some people feel she's too bossy."

"Yes, she just needs me to let her know when it's too much, and we're working together on that."

"The fact that you see her bossiness as something to be worked on, rather than just cutting her off and not dealing with it, is so wonderful to me. Usually the village doesn't operate like that."

"I see what you mean, but I know Edna can understand, and she does want to learn what is appropriate. Besides she knows I enjoy her."

I felt so happy, I wanted to sing.

"Look at this," I said, reading the recipe. "You heat the olive oil until it's hot but just short of smoking, and then you pour it over the salad, coating the leaves so it wilts them."

As we stood there, one of us pouring, the other turning leaves with tongs, it struck me how natural it was for me to be hanging out in the kitchen, cooking with a new friend who was now part of Edna's family. Edna and I had never had a mutual friend, someone who both appreciated and loved my sister, and who connected with me. Zalene understood how important Edna was to me. I had never felt this at home in the village.

When lunch was ready, we sat down together at the long, handmade wooden table: Edna and the five other villagers who lived in the house; Rebecca, Seth, and me; and Zalene and her family.

"Blessing on the meal," Edna said, as we all held hands.

Part 3

Chapter 24

For the next two years while Edna lived with Zalene, her asthma attacks virtually disappeared.

She also spent several weekends with us in the city, managing to take the bus on her own to Port Authority, where either Seth or I would be waiting for her. My sister especially enjoyed it when Seth picked her up and took her to McDonald's for vanilla shakes and Big Macs.

"Your sister might not think it's a great idea, but let's do it," he offered conspiratorially.

"I don't get to do that in the village; it's a good idea," Edna agreed.

Seth was also good at sitting with her at the computer, helping her learn how to send emails, something I would not have attempted. Edna was always game to try something new.

Alas, Rebecca did not look forward to her aunt's visits. As an only child, she was used to having my full attention. But with Edna there, she had to share me with a special kind of other child. In our small apartment, Edna was given Rebecca's room so she could spread out. As compensation, Rebecca was allowed to crawl into bed with us. But still she complained. And once when Edna went for a walk around the block on her own—a favorite activity of hers—I caught Rebecca and her friend Laura imitating Edna's gestures.

"What are you doing, how dare you do that," I shouted, losing all my therapeutic and mothering skills in an instant. "How would you feel if she walked in and saw you? This is my sister and your aunt."

"We were just playing," Rebecca protested.

"That wasn't playing!"

"Mommy, you're scaring me," my daughter said, running over to touch my arm. I had never spoken to her that way before.

"Look," I relented. "I know it's not easy for you to have her here. And you can always tell me how you feel if she's a pain. You know you can. But if you ever do that again, I'll go crazy." I put my arm around both girls and explained how I had grown up protecting Edna from this kind of behavior.

When Edna returned, Rebecca took her hand and said, "Let's read a story on the couch."

When Zalene's life circumstances changed and she left the village after two years, Edna's good health honeymoon ended. She gradually deteriorated, and there could be no more visits to me. Before long, I was drawn increasingly into her life. There were frequent phone calls and visits, sometimes to emergency rooms, as well as conversations with the care group at the village about how to manage my sister's illness. And though the responsibility felt both inevitable and natural, at times I resented it. I experienced the old conflict of caring deeply, yet wanting to push Edna away. I loved being a mother to my nine-year-old, going on class trips, watching her learn to ride a horse, and reveling in her outrageous but fabulous outfits. It was hard to switch my attention from my joyful, agile child to Edna, especially as questions began to arise about the wisdom of her remaining in the village. She seemed to have aged quickly, not uncommon in people with developmental disabilities. And her asthma, now chronic, was becoming unmanageable at the village, which lacked the 24/7 nursing care she needed. This reality was terrifying to me.

The village had been Edna's home for nearly forty years, and my parents and I had assumed it always would be her home. What's more, I blamed the coworkers for the progression of her disease. They'd been slow to realize the necessity of treating her as soon as she began to wheeze. Favoring homeopathic remedies over conventional medicine had led to a vicious cycle of trips to the emergency room, with Edna usually in a breathless panic.

At the same time, the use of steroid inhalers—the most effective way to treat asthma—was not an option. Edna couldn't tell the difference between an in- or an out-breath, and her hands shook when she tried to press the button to release the medicine. As a result, she was dependent on a much less efficient nebulizer that required her to lie down for half-hour periods while the medicine was pumped through the air. And though eventually the village leaders came to recognize more of Edna's needs, the side effects from the steroids made her vulnerable to brittle and broken bones, increased jitteriness, and heightened anxiety. My sister was no longer thriving.

The horrifying prospect of Edna in a nursing home loomed large. I couldn't imagine my sister, who lived where candles were lit at every meal, with organic food from the garden, living in an institution.

At a meeting of the care group, to which I was invited but Edna was not, the consensus was that the village could no longer provide the care she needed. In fact, it seemed as if it had already been decided that my sister had to leave.

"Edna gets so anxious about all the details in the house," I was told. "Everything becomes a calamity. This person was late for work, or that person forgot the eggs. We have prescribed a psychotropic, anti-anxiety medication for her, but it's not enough."

Yes, I thought, because it's about five years too late. Maybe the current scenario could have been avoided. But regardless, I'd already planned to take Edna to a pulmonary specialist in Manhattan.

I made eye contact with each member of the care committee and said, "Maybe there are treatment options we don't yet know about. Perhaps there are new drugs. If there's any way for her to continue living in the village, I want that to happen."

"We're struggling to keep Edna, but we understand your concern," was the surprising response. "If that feels important, why don't you go ahead and see what you can learn." I hadn't expected them to listen and give me this chance.

Two weeks later I returned to the village to pick up Edna and drive her to Manhattan for the appointment.

On the way, I asked her what it was like when she wheezed.

"It's hard at night."

I asked her why.

"I don't like to wake them up."

"But you have to," I said, noticing that I was starting to speed. "I'm sure they'd understand."

"I have to go upstairs, and I don't like to bother them."

"We'll figure this out," I assured her, not feeling at all confident that we would.

A heavily varnished blond wooden desk took up most of the doctor's office, and its gated window looked out on Park Avenue. With his impeccably clipped hair, tortoise shell glasses and white Oxford shirt, the doctor shook hands with each of us and then motioned us into beige upholstered chairs.

I explained the inhaler issue, along with the almost impossible task of describing Edna's life in the village.

He listened silently, his hands resting on the desk. "Of course, she'll need regular appointments with me, if she is to be my patient," he said finally, glancing at his watch.

"I don't think that's possible," I said. "We're here to see if there might be some new options for her to try. Isn't there anything you can offer her now?"

He flipped through the folder I'd brought from the village, and then asked Edna to stand so he could examine her. After briefly listening to her breathe, he agreed that she needed to be on steroids, even with all the side effects.

"Have you tried this kind of inhaler when she starts to wheeze?" he wondered, pulling something out of the drawer. "This is new, good for elderly people. Plus, it's easy to operate. You just put it in your mouth."

The word *elderly* hovered in the air. To this doctor, my younger sister, who was only fifty-five, was an infirm, elderly person.

Edna's head trembled when he inserted the inhaler into her mouth. Remarkably, she didn't have to do anything except tilt her head back to operate it. And it worked!

We drove back to Camphill singing every folk song we knew. There was a new weapon that could help my sister at night, so she didn't have to wake anyone up. I thought we had bought some time.

But it was too little, too late. Edna knew she had to leave Camphill. She lost weight, lost the inhaler, worried all the time, and sometimes reverted to her bossy self, nudging others if she decided they weren't setting the table correctly. What she needed to ease her mind was someone who would be there for her around the clock.

My sister was brave, ready to leave her home of nearly forty years. The awful nursing home smells, the fake cheer of the staff, the bleak hallways crawling with wheelchairs didn't faze her. Edna had no judgments, but I was frightened and enraged. How could my beautiful sister live in a sterile institution with no cows to pet in a barn?

What's more, without the buffer of the village, having Edna live in a nursing home would increase my level of responsibility. It would fall to me to monitor her care. Seth wasn't as solicitous of her as he used to be, no doubt because our relationship had become strained and distant. And though my father arranged for Edna to visit him for a weekend every few months, he relied on me to keep tabs on her. He welcomed my calls when I had concerns, but trusted me to know what was right for her.

"You are a wonderful sister," he would always say. "I'm so grateful for all you do."

Our little nuclear family was down to just Edna and me. I would be her sister-guardian, accompanying her on a life-changing journey filled with uncertainty.

The first decision was which nursing home, and where. After forty years of living in the country, should Edna move to a home in the city to be near me? But I'd be the only one visiting her—not a good choice for either of us. Yet, could she live far away all by herself?

"I want to live near the village, so I can do things like go to the Michaelmas Festival," Edna said in a clear voice, settling the matter. Her spiritual and psychic home was still the village, and she needed to live nearby so people would visit her and she could visit them. As important as I was to her, she had her own life.

I'd forgotten that it wasn't all up to me. Edna knew her own mind and could express her needs. We would learn together how to navigate her new life.

Chapter 25

The village care group found a decent nursing home in Great Barrington that was half an hour from Camphill. Edna had moved in a week before my first visit. I wanted to see how she was faring in her new home but dreaded going. I felt old guilty feelings, because her life was narrowing while mine flourished. And for her to live her last years in an institutional setting made me feel as if our family and society had failed her. Driving through the main street of town, glancing at restaurants, coffee shops, and vintage stores, I tried to spin a positive tale, picturing outings that could be fun. Then I hooked a sharp left under a bridge, climbed a hill, and turned into a long driveway flanked by a manicured lawn and shrubs. A sprawling, one-story brick building came into view. This was alien territory. I felt as if I had dropped from a parachute while on some bizarre mission, and through a twisted combination of accident and purposefulness, had landed at a spot on the map marked "nursing home."

Automatic doors slid open, revealing empty wheelchairs folded and stacked along a dark hallway. There was no sign of life. I found myself gripping a railing that ran the length of the wall, forcing myself to put one foot in front of the other. Turning the corner, I encountered an indescribable odor, perhaps air freshener mixed with urine. Continuing on, I came to an open doorway and looked inside. There was Edna, seated with three white-haired ladies at a table with a vase of artificial daisies. She was dressed in a raggedy sweater and mismatched socks. I choked back tears.

"This is Florence, Aida, and Bernice. They live on my floor," she said in an excited voice when she saw me.

Florence smiled and said, "How are you?" The other two didn't look up.

I glanced at Edna's plate and saw applesauce and half of a fish stick, which partially explained the odor in the overheated dining room.

"Let's see your room," I said, feeling nauseous.

As we walked down the hall, she greeted nurses' aides and people slumped in wheelchairs. My sister already knew everyone's name and was introducing me and encouraging me to say hello. I tried not to shrink inside myself. This wasn't the village. Edna's need to befriend everyone might not be so welcome, the way it had been all through our childhood, except at The Club.

Her room was small but, luckily, her roommate wasn't there. I felt relieved. At least the bedspread belonged to her. And though there were boxes still to be unpacked, her photos of Seth, Rebecca, our parents, and me were arranged on her one shelf.

"I want to help you unpack and make this cozy and see what you need," I said, in my *we can do this* voice.

"The nurses are very nice," she said.

"Do you get any fresh fruit here?" I asked, picturing the fish sticks and plastic bowls of canned fruit cocktail, each topped with a bright, chemically red cherry.

"We can have bananas at breakfast."

"How about if we go shopping and buy you some apples? Let's make a list and get stuff for your room. There are some antique stores near here. We could find you a desk so you'll have a nice place to write letters."

Leaving the parking lot, I realized that being so close to Great

Barrington might have advantages after the rural remoteness of Camphill. We had an escape. Edna loved going into stores. Our first stop was a secondhand shop where we tried on antique straw hats.

"That one looks good on you, Susie," she said.

"You are still the only one who calls me that," I said, hugging her.

In the back of a shop, we spotted a small, drop-down oak desk and a green Depression glass bowl for the apples I'd insisted on buying.

"It will be nice to have something fresh in your room," I told her.

"Fine," Edna said, and I realized I was way more concerned about her circumstances than she was. This wasn't *my* life, I reminded myself, and I had to find a way to accept her new reality.

We ate dinner in a candlelit Indian restaurant where she could order real seafood, her favorite. And after dinner, I carried the little desk down the long hallway to her room where it fit right under the window. Edna began rummaging through a box of papers and letters, going off into her own world. She loved sorting things out. At least now she had some drawers. Clearly, it was time for me to go.

My sister walked me back down the long corridor to the parking lot.

"I'll be back really soon," I promised, taking her hands in mine.

"I'm fine. Thanks for coming and helping me," she said, already turning away.

Goodbyes were never her strong point, but knowing that didn't make my departure any easier. I sobbed as I pulled out of the parking lot, and then spent the drive home making a mental to-do list: talk to the social worker, ask what would Edna be doing all day, how could she get to the village, could they arrange a taxi, would they call me if she was sick, how do we set up a private phone for her, and what could I do about her having fresh fruit all the time? And then it came to me: Fruit of the Month Club. She would be getting a surprise package, she would enjoy giving some away, and she could use the green bowl.

We were going to get through this.

❁

Over the next couple of months, things did fall into place. Because Edna was diagnosed as developmentally disabled, she was entitled to a one-on-one aide for ten hours a week. Bonnie was warm and energetic, and they planned activities together. Edna would call and report that they'd gone to a gym where she was learning to ride an exercise bike. Or they'd attended a weekly craft program for the developmentally disabled, or had visited the village. Bonnie even took Edna to visit an elderly client of hers who loved my sister and always asked for her to come. The Fruit of the Month started arriving, and I found a friendly taxi company that could pick her up and take her to places such as the local Christian Community Church, which was based on Rudolf Steiner principles. Then we realized that Edna could call for the cab herself; I just needed to pay the bill. And so one Saturday morning, she told me, she'd gone on her own to the green market in Great Barrington, where she'd bought raspberry jam. While she took advantage of the nursing home activities, she was also creating a life of her own. I couldn't believe it, yet her life in the nursing home was turning out to be more independent than it had been at the village. The big difference was that she got to decide which activities she wanted to pursue. At the village, so much had been organized for her. But now she had the support of 24-hour care, which relieved her anxiety and allowed her to try new things. Knowing she had more support, I could relax and even accept the nursing home as offering her new possibilities to grow. This was yet another welcome turn of the kaleidoscope!

I felt victorious. There was life after the village. I only wished my mother were alive to see how well Edna was managing.

Chapter 26

I was making a list of ingredients to buy for Thanksgiving dinner when the social worker from the nursing home called.

"We have a bit of a challenging situation developing with Edna, and I wanted to talk to you about it," she said, sounding upbeat. "You see Edna has been creating some disruptions here and. . . ."

We hadn't even passed the three-month mark. I felt shock waves go through me. My pen started making random circular marks on the pad.

"Well, and you know I'm very fond of Edna," she continued.

Sure, she liked her when everything was going well, and she was pleased that Edna was one of the few residents who could walk, talk, and eat by herself. But now the woman's voice dripped with phony professional sincerity.

Edna was being Edna, just trying to be helpful. But, to the staff at the home, she was bothering other patients, trying to get them to do things they didn't want to do, and when their families were visiting, she would go right up to them and make suggestions about what their loved ones needed. "And, well, in short, we've had some complaints."

Could my sister be evicted from a nursing home? Was that possible? I asked what she was suggesting.

"Well, we're thinking about it. She's been doing things like answering the phone at the nurses' station when no one is there, but we have been working on getting that to stop."

"You do know that in the village she was taught to help out and she's just trying to be useful," I said defensively.

They understood, explained the social worker, but Edna's behavior was interfering with their protocols and violating their practices.

"So where do we go from here?" I asked, fighting tears.

"I am checking with you, but our best solution is to move her to the Alzheimer's wing. That way she wouldn't have so much impact on people."

"What?" I was screaming. "Put her with people that she can't even talk to? And isn't that a locked floor? You'd punish her because her social skills are a little awkward?"

The unit was indeed locked, but Edna would be able to come and go and eat in the dining room and attend activities.

"So, you're not asking, you're telling me."

They were just trying it, she said, in that same relentless, upbeat voice.

I forced the scream down and told her I'd be up to visit Edna that weekend.

After ringing to have the locked door opened, I walked down the wheelchair-clogged hallway of the Alzheimer's wing, feeling like the little girl I'd been at the Club, pretending I was fine and grown-up enough to get through this. Then I saw Edna, her arm around a very frail, wispy-haired woman in a bathrobe, helping her to walk.

"It's fine, Martha, just a little farther and we will be in our room," she was saying when I caught up to her. She looked up, but before I could speak, she said, "This is my new roommate, Martha. You can shake hands with her."

"Hi, Martha," I said, reluctantly taking her hand.

Martha smiled sweetly. In that moment I knew that Edna was in the right place. She didn't care if these people had dementia. She didn't separate people into categories the way I did. And Martha and the others seemed to accept her involvement. She could do her work here. And her work was sacred. Although from the nursing home staff's point of view, Edna was being pushed out of the way, here she was free to help people who were able to receive her care. The arrangement was so perfect; it was almost beyond my comprehension. Because what it looked like on the surface had nothing to do with what it actually was. It felt to me that there was a much bigger force at work here, teaching me something that I was just dimly beginning to grasp. Edna, just being Edna, had landed on this floor. And now she could continue to be herself. She was on her own singular path that was unfolding just the way it needed to, regardless of my judgments. And though I could ease her way by visiting or by buying her a desk, I couldn't chart her course.

A few weeks later she called me up. "I went to an Arlo Guthrie concert. I went by myself and he sang 'City of New Orleans,' but not 'Alice's Restaurant.'"

"By yourself?"

"I called the taxi and told them to pick me up, and then they came back right in front of the church where the concert was and took me home after it was over."

I asked how she knew about it.

"It was in the *Berkshire Eagle*, so I called the number and they said they had tickets."

And that was my remarkable sister. How many people go to concerts by themselves? Not something I remember doing. And how many people living in the Alzheimer's wing of a nursing home call taxis and go to concerts by themselves? Well, that was just off the charts.

❀

What I learned from Edna helped me handle the new big shift in my life. After many years of us each accommodating the age difference in our marriage, Seth and I realized that we needed to separate. At 58 I was happy being a mom to a fourteen-year-old, working hard with patients, cooking dinner for friends, and anticipating slowing down. At twenty-five, Seth had sacrificed his dream of becoming an actor or film editor in order to earn a stable income doing work he barely tolerated. Now in his forties, he was bursting to follow his dream. Yet, loving our family of three and dreading how separation would affect our sensitive teenager, we tried but failed to resurrect a romance that had slipped away. We had been together almost seventeen years; this was the marriage that was supposed to last. But that ideal no longer fit our reality.

Leaving a third marriage, I could have felt shame. I could have felt like a failure and blamed myself for being unrealistic from the beginning. But, as with Edna, what our separation looked like on the surface was not the way it was. This was a different way of leaving.

Seth and I had lived a full life, and I was eternally grateful to him. In our unconventional marriage, we had brought up a beautiful, talented, and loving daughter. We had sung lullabies, backpacked in Montana, and camped out at Camphill. We had come together for a wonderful purpose, but our relationship was no longer sustainable as a marriage.

I had done my best to make my dream of marriage with children a reality, with compromises, risks, and unknowns. Whatever my life looked like from the outside, I no longer cared. No longer feeling defective or having to prove something, or aspiring to be part of some inner circle, I was proud of my choices.

Seth and I remained amicable and thought it best for Rebecca to live with me in the familiarity of our apartment. But he moved just three blocks away and spent many evenings coming over and cooking Rebecca dinner while I was working. And she spent weekends at his place.

Our arrangement was fluid and worked well. But even in the best of circumstances, divorce is devastating. Although Rebecca didn't confide in me, I knew she was hurting. Two things helped: I found her a wonderful therapist, and I bought her a horse. Riding had been her passion all through childhood, and it had always soothed her to be around horses. But to buy and care for a horse had been out of our range. Now, through a complicated set of circumstances, an opportunity opened up that was affordable. My father offered funds to buy Killian, and I found a way to stable him upstate, only two hours from Manhattan. Muffy, the lovely young woman who owned the barn, was interested in working with teenagers who were a bit vulnerable. On many weekends during her high school years, Rebecca took the bus upstate to be at the barn with Killian, riding, grooming, and even competing. And Muffy became an important role model and trusted friend to our daughter.

Chapter 27

Edna continued to surprise me with her wisdom and impact on people. Two instances stand out.

The first occurred at our father's funeral. For almost ten years after my mother died, my father lived a rich life in the community, making new friends, exploring the area, and even getting his hands dirty in a pottery class. He and his friends called themselves the "jet set," a sea change from the way my reserved father had lived most of his life. On occasion, he and a friend would even drive up to visit Edna for the day.

In his last year, although in general good health, he had gradually become weaker until he sometimes needed a wheelchair to get around. All his life my father had loved to walk and hike in nature. "When someone has to push me, it's the end," he said to me.

I knew it was coming soon.

Shortly before his ninety-sixth birthday, he died in his bed. I was lucky to be with him, rubbing his feet and holding his hand. Some minutes before he breathed his last, I heard him say, "Get me over." I mistakenly thought he wanted to be turned. But when I realized what he meant, I just held his hand and breathed with him until the last breath.

We held the memorial in the community auditorium, a light-filled room packed with all his friends and the coworkers who had cared for him.

Several people spoke about how considerate and helpful my father had been. He had saved *New Yorker* magazines for one, lent his car to another, and been a steady, wonderful friend going places with many others. A coworker mentioned that on his last day, he had expressed some impatience about getting a drink of water. When she brought a glass in to him, he had apologized. He'd told her he knew he was impatient and was working on it.

"He was still trying on his last day," she said.

At the memorial I talked about how my father had always had my back and how much he loved me.

Then Edna slowly walked up to the front of the room.

She looked out at everyone and, in her clear unwavering way, said, "I think my father would want to thank you for taking such good care of him. He had a wonderful life here."

All rustling ceased. I glanced around me to see people nodding and smiling.

What my sister had said was perfect. It was exactly what my father would have wanted to say, it was what everyone needed to hear, and it came from a selfless place.

I was so proud and grateful for Edna's consciousness.

The second event, involving our uncle, was even more dramatic.

When we were children, Uncle Ernst was our least favorite relative. My mother's younger brother, Ernst was a disgruntled curmudgeon who would speak to us in German and then be critical when we didn't understand. He would get angry with me because I wasn't interested in current events. Edna, he didn't bother with much. We both preferred Aunt Hannah, who would come into our room and play dolls with us. Both Uncle Ernst and Aunt Hannah had been traumatized by the war. Our uncle had been sent to New York by his parents to live with distant relatives when he was only sixteen. Our aunt lived with the reality of the death of her parents at Auschwitz. That's the only reason I can think of to explain why, in the forty years Edna was at Camphill, our uncle and aunt had visited her only once. Perhaps the whole setting was more than they could deal with. In our family lore, my parents deeply resented their lack of emotional support. Though Edna was certainly aware of their absence and would have enjoyed some visits, she didn't hold it against them.

After Aunt Hannah died and Ernst was in his eighties, Edna began calling him once a week. "It's good to call, because he's alone now," she said, when I tried to point out how mean he had been to us.

I resolved to call him, too, but often went months before picking up the phone.

A year after my father died, I received a call from Uncle Ernst's caregiver. Now quite frail and using a walker, he was insisting that he wanted to visit Edna. That meant taking a train from Washington, DC, to Albany, and hiring a car service to drive him from there to Great Barrington.

He was brusque on the phone. "I just want to know Edna's address." I was clearly not his favorite niece.

The following week, Edna called in the evening. She had taken a cab to the motel where Ernst was staying. He had taken her to Kmart, bought her a dress and some chocolates, and then they had eaten dinner at an Italian restaurant.

"It was nice to see him," she reported.

At six the next morning, I received a call from his distraught caretaker. Ernst had woken up, keeled over, and died in the motel room bed.

"I couldn't do anything to stop him," she worried.

"He had to do this. It's not your fault," I said, trying to comfort her and promising that I would help her figure out the logistics of getting his body back to Washington.

Indeed, it appeared that he did have to see Edna before he died. Her love, expressed by consistent phone calls, had touched him and jogged his conscience. In his last act on earth, he was impelled to rectify years of neglect.

Edna took the news with equanimity.

"It was good that he came."

Chapter 28

Around the same time, I received an extraordinary gift.

Taking a midday break from seeing clients, I was rifling through magazines as I sat in the waiting room before my annual gynecological checkup. For me, this was always an extra yearly spotlight on, "You have no uterus," and at age fifty-nine, I still needed to steel myself for it. In the examining room, the nurse, inevitably new since my last visit, would come in and ask the usual question: "So when did you have your last period?" And I would say, "If you look at my record, you'll see that I have this condition, so I never menstruated." But then, luckily, I would anticipate seeing Dr. Ella, an old-world Hungarian, who would put her arm around me and say, "How are you? Let's just have a look at your breasts."

But Dr. Ella had died, and today I had an appointment with the new, younger doctor. Starting over again, I felt myself contracting and flattening like a pancake.

The nurse appeared in the doorway, motioned me into the examination room and, to my relief, she had no questions. She only wanted to take my blood pressure. Then a young woman with wavy shoulder-length hair and deep orange lipstick entered the room. Her white coat open, she was curvaceous in a dark, tight-fitting suit. Making eye contact, she smiled, introduced herself as Dr. Nielson, and asked if I was here for a routine checkup.

"Yup," I said, averting my eyes. "I only need the mammogram referral, because I never menstruated and was born without a uterus," I said, my inner dukes up.

"Oh," she said, no longer smiling, but still looking directly at me. "That sounds like it could be MRKH syndrome."

"MRKH syndrome?" I repeated slowly. "What is that? Nobody has ever said that to me."

She looked surprised. "Let's just take a look at your chart for a moment."

As she read, I held my breath and watched her finger scroll down the page.

"Sure, that's what it is."

I swallowed hard, starting to feel woozy. My mind was not keeping up with her words.

She explained that MRKH was a rare condition and that one in four thousand women have it. There were some variations, with some people having kidney problems and others having no uterus, and still others having partial ones.

"I'll get the book and show you, if you want."

"Definitely, that would be good," I said, feeling wobbly.

How is that possible? I thought. I'm almost sixty, and I don't know anything about this. I can't believe it. One in four thousand: that's a lot of women. I always thought I was a complete anomaly, maybe one in a million, or god knows what. But one in four thousand is an actual statistic.

I flashed back to being fifteen and the doctor's pronouncement: "You'll never menstruate. You'll need surgery."

Was I missing something? Had they told my mother? No, nothing like this was ever said, I was sure of it. Nobody ever told me my condition had a name.

"Here it is," Dr. Nielson said, walking back into the room. She placed the book on my knees. MRKH, named after four doctors: Mayer-Rokitansky-Küster-Hauser syndrome, identified in 1838.

It goes that far back, and they didn't tell me? How could this be?

I followed the doctor's finger down the page: "Usually discovered during teenage years at failure to menstruate, possible treatments: dilation or surgery to create a proper vaginal opening." That was me in print, on the page.

"Dilation, that was what I did," I said, grabbing onto the word and, for the first time, looking directly at the doctor.

"That was good that you didn't need surgery," she said.

Thank you, Mom, I thought, for taking me to a second doctor. I wish you were here with me now. We could know this together.

Feeling even more stunned, I read on: "Other names: Mullerian agenesis, vaginal agenesis. Etiology unclear: caused by failure of reproductive ducts to develop in the early stages of pregnancy."

"You should go online," Dr. Nielson said calmly, eyeing me. "I think you'll find out more, and there might even be support groups."

Support groups? After all this time? For what?

"How come no one ever told me this?" I said, with a sudden spurt of anger. "All these years that I haven't known. I've been to several doctors over the years, had a hysterectomy in my fifties because a doctor felt a mass there, so I had a hysterectomy. The mass was my rudimentary uterus. It was just me. Not cancer. But the doctor said it was good it was out, because you never know, it could cause trouble. Not one person ever told me my condition had a name."

"I can't tell you why," she answered.

"This whole thing is unbelievable." I said, trawling for words and finding none. I was fifty-nine. My disability had a name. It was truly crazy, this sinister sounding anagram of four surnames. I was going to memorize them and imprint them in my brain. That way I could rattle the whole thing off to whomever I told.

"Do you have a piece of paper and a pen?" I asked.

She handed me the pad and I printed the four names in capital letters. "This means so much to me. Have you ever seen someone else with this?"

She told me she'd studied it, but hadn't actually seen it before.

"Well, then, I can be your first," I said, half-smiling and reaching out my hand to shake hers.

There was the slightest pause and then she took my hand. "That's true," she said, but quickly let go and began writing in the chart. "So, here's your mammogram referral, and I'll see you in a year." And with that she left. I stared dumbfounded at the referral in one hand and the paper with the names in the other. I exhaled, wishing she could have said something that showed she understood how momentous this was for me. Still, her businesslike manner was a small price to pay for the gift she had just given to me.

In a daze I walked slowly down First Avenue, trying to understand what this meant. Something did feel different, though by the time I got this information I was already at peace with being me. And yet, knowing there were others like me was a sea change. No longer an invisible anomaly, my syndrome existed in a book, and I could join a special sisterhood of women of all ages, all over the world.

In time I would become part of an active online community, facilitate in-person support groups in several cities, and be a therapist to a young woman diagnosed with MRKH who struggled with self-esteem issues. I would learn about the new technology of extracting our eggs, so they could be fertilized and lead to a viable pregnancy through surrogacy, and I would embrace a woman who had had two children that way. There would even be the new frontier of uterus transplants.

But for now, it was time to go online to see who was out there.

Chapter 29

Something was going terribly wrong with Edna, now fifty-nine, during Christmas week, the worst possible time to be sick in a nursing home. Unusual for her, she had called me complaining of pain. Learning that her regular doctor was on vacation, I needed to see for myself what was going on.

"The pain was all over," she said, when I moved my chair close to the bed and took her hand. "But it's better now."

The LPN appeared and asked to speak with me. She reported that Edna had been very upset and they'd had to have someone sit with her all day because she had been hitting and scratching herself.

"Why?" I asked. "I don't get it. Why was she doing that? She looks terribly thin and pale."

The nurse told me Edna had been very agitated, which could have been a side effect of the steroids she was taking for asthma. Then she flipped through the chart and mentioned that Edna had complained of a toothache and needed to see a dentist. This was probably just another of her many teeth that needed to be pulled, because my sister had never been good at coordinating her fingers for dental hygiene.

When I asked why she hadn't seen the dentist, the nurse said he was on vacation.

"But she's been in terrible pain. Isn't there another dentist we could see? This is crazy."

The nurse told me to calm down, adding that Edna had already been examined at the emergency room, but the doctor couldn't find anything wrong. He'd given her painkillers and she was feeling much better.

"This doesn't feel good to me," I insisted. "What about her asthma? She's had severe attacks in the past. Is there a doctor I could speak to?"

She promised to ask the doctor for another consult as soon as possible.

"When is the dentist back?" I pressed.

"We have Edna scheduled for the first week in January, first appointment when he gets back," she said, flashing me a relax-I'm-on-top-of-this smile.

I felt a little better. I knew this nurse really cared about Edna and checked on her frequently. It seemed that the nursing home staff was doing what they could to make her comfortable, and a doctor had seen her.

I went back to her room and asked her to tell me what had happened.

"I told the nurse the pain was so much and I needed to go to the emergency room."

"Good for you," I said. "And then what happened?"

"They took me there and the doctor looked in my mouth and took my temperature. He said I would feel better soon. And I do feel better, because he gave me some medicine."

"But why did someone have to sit with you all day?"

"They didn't want to leave me alone."

"You were hurting yourself."

"The pain was so bad."

"Well it's good you said you needed to go to the hospital. I'm going to talk to the doctor. And the tooth will come out soon. We'll sort this out," I assured her, trying to calm us both. My sister looked so vulnerable. Her glasses were too big for her face, and her skin was raw from scratching. I had never seen her like this. I took her hand and held it for a long time.

"Look, I brought you something to look at from your bed" I said, changing the subject. I'll open it," I added, when she started to struggle with the wrapping paper. Inside there was a clear plastic cylinder with a red tray wrapped around it.

"A bird feeder," Edna said.

"I brought seed, too. I'm going to hang it outside your window and we can watch the birds together.

"How nice," she said, smiling a little.

"I'll be right back."

Walking down the hall, I paused to breathe. I didn't know what else to do for Edna, but at least the bird feeder would give her some pleasure.

I waved to her from the courtyard and she waved back. I poured the birdseed into the feeder and carefully hung it on the low branch of a tree right outside her window. By the time I got back to her room, two crows were already guzzling down their lunch.

We sat for a while watching the birds

"This is going to be okay," I said. "We just have to give it some time."

"Okay," she said.

"I'm going home now, but I'll call back tonight and make sure the doctor has seen you, and you can call me anytime."

"I love you," she said.

"I love you back," I said, choking off tears. I was surprised, because that wasn't something Edna would ordinarily say.

I stroked her face and took her hand in mine one more time before I left.

❀

Two days later, a doctor from the Great Barrington Hospital emergency department phoned to say that Edna had arrived in critical condition and had been intubated, and I should come.

When I arrived, a nurse was sitting by Edna's bed, holding her hand. I stood on the other side of the bed. My sister's eyes were closed, her hair flattened across her forehead, her face drained of all color.

"She's conscious," the nurse said, smiling reassuringly. "Edna, your sister's here now."

Her glasses and partial dentures had been left behind at the nursing home, so she couldn't see well and it was hard to understand what she was saying. Still, she was trying to talk.

"You're great, thank you," Edna mumbled to the nurse.

"Your sister is so special and courageous," the nurse said to me.

I felt as if I was about to crumble. I wanted to cry, but couldn't.

Words to a song we both loved floated up, and I sang, "The water is wide, and I cannot cross over, and neither have I wings to fly. Build me a boat that can carry two, and both shall row, my love and I."

I sensed her listening and told myself she would come through this. I just needed to get her stuff from the nursing home so she could see and talk.

"I'm going to get your glasses and teeth, so we can sing some more. I'll be right back," I said, gripping her hand in mine.

Grabbing my jacket, running to my car, gunning it for the ten-minute drive back to the home, flying down the hall to Edna's room. Her bed was unmade, the tray table next to it was pushed aside, a copy of *Reader's Digest* and her glasses on the table, along with a glass of water that held her teeth. Grabbing them, running back the other way, gunning the car again, sitting by her side, the nurse helping her put in her teeth.

"Now we can be in business, and sing. How about "Kisses Sweeter than Wine?"

She nodded, but her eyes closed and she drifted off.

The doctor had come in and was motioning to me into his office.

"What is her prognosis?" I asked.

He told me he wasn't sure, that we would have to see how she did overnight. Her body was in sepsis. She was fifty-nine, but from all the steroids she'd taken, she had the body and lungs of an eighty-year-old.

"If we hadn't intubated her, she would have died. But wait," he asked. "Does she have a living will?"

"Living will?" Edna was way too young to die. "No, I don't think so," I said. "I'm her legal guardian. Oh, my god, no, we haven't thought in those terms. Our attorney didn't advise us about that."

"Well, if you are her legal guardian, do you have those papers with you?"

I had rushed out of the house without thinking. He told me I'd have to talk to the hospital administrator.

"Listen," I said, gazing directly into his eyes, "I'm her sister and her legal guardian. Clearly, you can see she is mentally challenged. Please don't send me all over the place."

He paused. "You might want to consider a Do Not Resuscitate order."

She might not make it and I was being called upon to make choices about living and dying. What would she want? What would my parents want? Both of them had died at home with peace and dignity. We would all want that for Edna. But now, she, the most vulnerable of us all, was lying in a hospital bed, prey to god knows what kind of invasive procedures.

"Yes, I want to sign that. No more suffering. It's enough."

He suggested I go back to my motel and return the next morning.

Not ten minutes later, as I lay on the soft Day's Inn bed, the phone rang.

It was the nurse. "I'm so sorry, she passed."

Stars fell through a black hole.

Edna was gone.

✿

The nurse who had been so loving was waiting for me at the nurses' station.

"I didn't want to leave until you came. She breathed her last peacefully," she said.

The woman took my arm, gently led me into Edna's room, and stepped back. Forcing myself to look for one long moment, my eyes fixed on a pale face with gray wisps of hair stuck to it. It was my sister's face, but it wasn't her. I went numb.

"You've been so wonderful," I said to the nurse, "but I can't stay here."

"I understand. I wanted to tell you that your sister had a special quality of gentleness that I felt all the time I was with her."

"That's amazing. Even though you only were with her from yesterday until tonight, I could tell how important you became to Edna. I'm so glad you were there." I felt embraced and held by this woman who had experienced and appreciated Edna's essence.

I asked her how it had happened so fast.

"I sit with many people who are passing, and it's hard to say. But she had seen you, and I think she was ready."

I turned and walked out of the room and found my way to the doctor's office. "How come it happened so fast?" I repeated to the doctor.

"I really can't tell you. The infection spread from an undiagnosed dental infection. And she was very fragile; her body couldn't fight it. That can happen. I'm sorry. By the time she got to this hospital, it was too late. We couldn't save her."

"Dental infection?" I couldn't believe what I was hearing. "Oh, my god, you do know that she went to the hospital in Pittsfield and they just gave her pain medication. And they never even tested her for an infection. This is insane."

"I saw that on the record," he nodded. "If you do an autopsy, you'll know for sure the cause of death. This is just our diagnosis, based on what we know."

"If I were going to speak to an attorney," I said carefully, monitoring the intense rage curling through me, "I would need an autopsy."

"An autopsy will give you the cause of death," he repeated.

I have to call the village, I thought. Edna would want to have all the rites of passing that the village performed, and I wasn't sure an autopsy would be possible.

Numb, my mind swirling, I stumbled out of the room. Call the village, get her things out of the nursing home, and call everyone in my life, maybe an attorney.

Edna had known she was dying. She just couldn't articulate it in a way that would make people listen. They had shushed her up with pain meds. But now I understood why she had told me she loved me when I'd left her at the home a few days before. Now I was hearing her. Now I understood why she had been hitting herself. A deadly infection was seeping through her body and she had tried to tell the doctors. She had insisted on going to the emergency room. But she could only advocate so far for herself. She couldn't scream out, I'm in pain, there's something really wrong. Don't just give me pain medication. And I had yelled at the doctors about her asthma because it could be deadly. Edna's teeth were not on my radar. I hadn't known her body was so frail that she could die from a toothache.

Chapter 30

When I phoned the village, Margrit, a coworker who had known Edna for many years, immediately declared, "Of course, we want her to be buried here in the village. It's her home."

Margrit's response washed over me like a soothing balm. Until that moment, I'd been either numb or drowning in replays of how I had failed to understand how precarious my sister's life was.

"I'm so happy to hear that," I said. "That feels right to me." And then I unburdened myself and recounted the story about malpractice and a potential lawsuit.

"If she's here," Margrit responded, "we would want her body to be as it is. You see, she'll be in full view in her casket for three days so everyone in the village can come and be with her. Her casket will be laid on dry ice to keep her body in its natural state, because we don't use embalming."

"So, an autopsy wouldn't fit?"

"No. Susan, I can't advise you about a lawsuit, but this thought might help. In the village we would say the infection was the occasion, but not the cause of her death."

"Not sure what that means," I said.

"She had a destiny, her time here was complete, and she was ready to cross the threshold."

"And the infection was just the way her death happened, like the means?" I asked.

"That's one way to put it."

This idea upended all of Western medicine and my previously held ideas about death and dying, cause and effect. Though familiar with reincarnation, I had not understood its connection to the cause of physical death, which believers view as a miniscule part of an unknowable, invisible process. Hearing what Margrit was saying, I felt as if I were being released from a burden. There seemed to be a much larger way to hold all of these recent, horrific events.

"Yes," I said, "I would very much like Edna to be buried at Camphill."

Margrit told me to come to the village and they would take care of everything.

I wanted the villagers to join me in being with Edna over the next days. She would have a loving send-off. There could be peacefulness and release. Perhaps her work really was complete. She had told her helper, Bonnie, this had been the best year of her life. So maybe this was truly the right time for her to leave.

But mentally I flipped back through her history of pain, and the ignorance and neglect surrounding her care. All her life Edna had been misdiagnosed and misunderstood, even as she was dying. Could I have done something more? I felt consumed with guilt over not grasping the seriousness of her dental issues. I could have yelled louder, demanded something more at the nursing home.

Still, I tried to take in the spiritual view. Maybe it was true; maybe Edna was finished with her work and her death had nothing to do with me. This idea could help me with the same lessons I'd been learning since she'd moved to the nursing home. My sister had lived her own life, and she lived her own death, and I couldn't change that any more than I could have stopped kids from making fun of her on the playground in elementary school. I wasn't there at the moment of her death; I had missed that boat. But we had rowed together in the boat of love when I sang to her. And nothing else really mattered.

For three days before the memorial service, Edna was laid out in the Crypt. This was a special room in Fountain Hall where all village festivals and community events took place. But for now it was just me living in the embrace of the community.

Opening a door I had never noticed before, I crept down a flight of stairs and opened another door to a smallish room lit with white tapers. A woman I didn't know sat near the door and was keeping vigil, her hands folded in the lap of her ankle-length skirt. I glanced toward the middle of the room and noticed white roses at one end of the casket, which was set on a low wooden table. As I inched toward it, I saw that my sister was laid out in her favorite blue batik Indonesian blouse and skirt, the outfit I'd chosen from the clothes I had stuffed into a plastic bag when I was clearing out her room.

My eyes half closed, I moved closer to the casket until I could touch her, and when I opened my eyes wide, I gasped. There in front of me was the face of a beautiful, strong, deeply intelligent woman, a face at peace, a face filled with wisdom. So beautiful and so womanly, with such a sense of wholeness. I stood there, rooted, entranced in a moment of such unbelievable and untranslatable knowing. Because this was my sister, and I totally recognized and knew her.

Here was Edna, the person she would have been if she hadn't been handicapped by a brain injury during birth. And yet, I thought, gazing at her, her life was much more than that; it wasn't about who she would have been if she hadn't had all the challenges of her disability. The strength reflected in her face included all of her struggles with her disabilities and all of her efforts to be everything she could be. Throughout her life, there was so much Edna couldn't share with me.

She didn't often express her feelings, and abstract concepts were difficult. But I always knew how hard she struggled to be recognized, to be as independent as possible. In her now there was openness. All of her was present: struggle, acceptance, and the sense of a life lived fully.

From the time I was a little girl, I tried to imagine Edna the way she would have been if she weren't disabled, and what our lives would have been like. Sometimes I pictured her as very popular and pretty, because even though she didn't understand social cues, she was always so friendly. But now there was no need to fantasize anything, because here was the person who had always been there for me. My steadfast and faithful sister. Even though for much of our lives we hadn't been physically together, standing there I felt the strength and love she had offered me all my life. Seeing her in her wholeness, I felt so light; we had both been released. Did you know how important you were to me? You surely did. All this time I've been your guardian, it's you who have been mine.

Chapter 31

ONE EARLY SPRING afternoon about a year and a half after Edna died, I was the first to arrive at the small burial ground on a gentle hill overlooking a pond in the village. This was the spot where we would have a simple ceremony to commemorate her gravestone. The stone was small and rectangular, engraved with Edna's name and the dates of her birth and death. It was set horizontally into the earth near about fifteen other graves.

I knelt down and brushed away pine needles and a few of last year's brown leaves so that the engraving was visible: Edna Wile, October 23, 1945–January 3, 2004. At first that looked fine, but then something was not quite right. My sister's full name was Edna Jane Wile, something the village didn't know. She was Edna Jane, and I was Susan Harriet, and there were times when we called each other that, just because we felt like it. Now it was only me who would know my sister's full name.

As I kept kneeling, a small ant meandered across her birth date, taking its time, going wherever it was meant to go. And for that moment of watching this small creature, I had a dawning sense of gentle openness and trust in my own life's process. Edna had moved on in the cycle of her life. She was home. Our relationship felt secure and enduring. And this was the one place I could always come to be with her, to draw strength.

"Edna Jane," I said quietly, but out loud. "Guess what? My inner problem about not getting my period or having children has a name. It's called MRKH. Not that this would matter to you at all. I know I'm totally fine to you."

"Interesting," I could hear her say.

"Just needed to tell you," I said, picking up a leaf.

Twirling it in my hand, I remembered how she always sent me leaves in her autumn letters.

I let the leaf go and it drifted down to a space next to Edna's stone. The thought slid in that this space could be for me. I was aware that there were a few family members buried next to their loved ones. It felt scary to imagine my own burial, but comforting to imagine being together again in this way. I would need to sit with this in the coming months and revisit it.

People were gathering in silence, coworkers with whom Edna had lived, and villagers, many now with gray hair. I noticed Bill standing a little apart from everyone. I walked over to be next to him.

We sang a couple of songs, and the suggestion was made for us to remain in silence until someone was moved to speak. It was a cloudy day, but trees were unfurling leaves of the lightest green, which shone through the gray.

It was a peaceful silence. Bill spoke into it.

"Edna was my girlfriend."

Everyone turned toward him.

"I miss her a lot." And that was all he said.

Bill never expressed feelings. A year ago at Edna's memorial service, one after another of the villagers, some whose speech was barely intelligible, had gotten up and acknowledged how Edna had sung to them or brought them flowers when they were sick, or how they had taken walks together. Bill had remained silent. Now it felt like I had just won a landslide of change from a slot machine, and I hadn't even put in a quarter.

I walked over to him and said, "Bill, you were Edna's boyfriend."

"I miss Edna Wile," he answered.

"I miss her, too," I said. "And you know what? When I come up here, I want to see you."

"You could just come on up here," he said and nodded.

"I definitely will," I said, tearing up.

Even though as time went on, they didn't spend much time together, Edna and Bill had had an enduring bond that lasted much longer than any of my intimate relationships. And after she'd moved into the nursing home, Edna mentioned that Bill hadn't come to visit her.

I asked her if she was angry.

"He should come," she answered.

"Have you thought of calling him?"

"Not really," she said.

"Why not?"

"No, Susan, he should know."

There was so much that neither Edna nor Bill could articulate to each other. But they had loved one another all these years. I wished there could have been help for them to express their feelings. But that hadn't happened, and it was time to accept the truth of it. In the "real" world, Bill would have been my brother-in-law. No, I corrected myself, this is the real world and he is my brother-in-law. And this Christmas I will look for a book on trains to send to him. He'll like that.

I wanted so much to tell this to Edna. Then suddenly I felt her presence. Her face was cocked a little sideways, and she wore a funny hat that didn't fit, but her voice was clear and her eyes steady, and I didn't have to say anything, because she was already saying to me, "I know it, I know it."

Edna, my sister, soul mate, and teacher for life. Always broken, forever whole.

Epilogue

On a July evening, I was strolling through Grand Central Station after a long day of listening to clients. I was early for my train to Westchester, where I now lived with Neal, a solid, big-hearted man I'd met online. He worked for IBM but was thinking of retiring. On our second date, I had told him about Edna's life, and right away he'd expressed interest in visiting the village, just to get to know me better. I had opened my heart once more, our relationship had bloomed, and we were even thinking of marriage. It would be my fourth. Sometimes I couldn't believe how a studious Jewish girl from Queens would end up with an Elizabeth Taylor lifestyle, but I tried not to judge myself. It had taken me that many tries to find an intimate, abiding relationship.

A young woman brushed past me. She carried a backpack, her sunglasses were propped on her head, and she wore tall boots with a short skirt. Her confident energy reminded me of Rebecca, now pursuing her passion in studio art at Alfred University. With my daughter settled, I was musing that this might be the right time to get married, when my eye caught a green swirl near the information booth. Drawn to it, I edged closer. The swirl was a group of people in green T-shirts in a cordoned-off area.

There were children in wheelchairs next to others who stood in off-kilter, slouching postures. Some were rocking, others were gesticulating with their hands, and some sat with their heads hanging over the sides of their chairs.

I moved closer. Young, fit-looking women and men accompanied each child. I could see the words "Camp Hope" written across the back of every T-shirt. I wanted to run for my train, but I just stood there, mesmerized. The scene was unbearably familiar. And so was my response: wanting to stay and stare, and wanting to run. My eyes traveled from one counselor to another, watching each one try to engage and connect with their charge. Some of the counselors were singing or playing a clapping game, another was brushing something away from a child's chin. The people in green T-shirts were smiling. One young man with long hair in a ponytail was letting a girl pull it. Another young woman was putting her sunglasses on a little girl who wore braids tied with bows.

I turned around and observed throngs of people rushing for their trains. They carried briefcases and some clacked along in high heels. Nobody stopped or paid attention and I thought: we're invisible. All these people can't see us. It's magic. This scene would only be visible to those who really want to understand, and most people don't.

I turned back to this little world of kids whose mothers and fathers had dressed them and packed their suitcases, because they, too, had wishes and dreams for their children. They, too, wanted them to have fun, to laugh and have friends, like other children. And they were. Just like other children, they were laughing at being tickled and acting silly.

Without warning, I began to weep.

There we were again, all of us, my father and mother, Edna and me. We were wearing green T-shirts that read Camp Hope, holding hands in our wheelchairs as we waited for our train. And I wasn't a therapist going home to Westchester, I was a little girl who wanted to be a counselor in a green T-shirt, and I was a little girl who wanted to find a counselor in a green T-shirt to take care of me, and for all of us, so we could laugh and be tickled.

What was it that I needed to learn from this scene?

And then, there it was in front of me, so obvious but true.

Camp Hope was the kaleidoscope of my entire life. When I held it one way I could see and feel all the wheelchair wounds that could hurt and scream *deficit, inadequate.* But turning the kaleidoscope a fraction of an inch, I could see people caring and being cared for, one braid pull at a time, loving and being loved, a circle of giving and receiving. Each view was a reality that held truth, and each was an inseparable part of the other.

I needed to hold it all. And now I could, because with each wound, people like Dr. Falk had cared about me. And from each wound I, too, had learned to love, one braid pull at a time. I was who I was, and there was nothing I would ever want to change.

Our family had found so many different kinds of Camp Hopes with counselors in green T-shirts, each of whom had offered us wisdom and comfort. All of us together, and each of us separately, had been willing to climb the steps to get on these trains, which sometimes seemed to be going in crazy or wrong directions. I thought of how open my parents had been to Camphill, and how my mother had insisted on finding a second doctor for me, how Edna had made herself a real home in the nursing home, how I knew I had to leave marriages, and the journey of how Rebecca came to me.

So much bravery and beauty in the jagged edges, in the unexpected, crooked paths of all these crisscrossing tracks.

I stood there a while longer, listening to the clicking of people's footsteps around me, smiling at my sisters and brothers in green T-shirts. And then I turned and headed to Track 28 to catch my train home.

ACKNOWLEDGMENTS

THANK YOU, PAUL Cooper, for encouraging me to write the chapter "Coming Home to Wholeness," in the book you edited, *Into the Mountain Stream*. That's how I got the first inkling that there was more to say.

Three incredible mentors showed up when I needed them. Kimberlee Auerbach Berlin, you found the seeds in your memoir writing class and insisted they could grow and bloom. You laughed and cried with me as the stories evolved into a book. Your generous, wise, and nurturing soul accompanied me and has meant more than I could ever express. Mark Matousek, you helped me understand the need for a more coherent narrative voice. Your metaphor of a cake with wonderful ingredients that needed to be baked, sustained me through several rewrites. So much gratitude! And Barbara Graham, your honest feedback, insight, and collaboration have been utterly invaluable. You helped me find the narrative voice of my older self. And then you stayed with me through yet another painful rewrite of slashing and rearranging to find the true story of Edna and me. Your insistence that I could bring my writing to another level is a priceless gift.

To all my friends who read various versions, many bows to you for cheering me along: Jill Stultz, Betsy Hallerman, Anne Shollar, Stephanie Stavinsky, Rick Burnett, Robin Kappy, Eileen Kaufman,

Jenny Ross, Judy Tarr, and Jude Cobb. Jude, who shared a similar sibling, many thanks for the conversations filled with compassion and insight. Special shout out to Robin my all-around pal and fellow artist. And countless other friends believed in me and always asked how it was going through years of work. Thank you.

To the cabin in Shandaken that offers solitude, fires and wildflowers:

To my practice of Focusing that invites me go deeper and find just the right words:

To my Zen practice of moment to moment presence:

Boundless thanks!

To Brooke Warner and She Writes Press, all my appreciation for publishing my book.

To Caitlin Hamilton Summie, many thanks for helping to usher it into the world.

Mom, your intention and dedication in the unpublished book you wrote about Edna now lives in mine.

Dad, your love and pride in my accomplishments are always with me.

Neal, my warm, loving husband, steadfast in your support. You read every word more than once and held me through whining and tears. I learn from your love every day!

Rebecca, my daughter, you can make me laugh like nobody else. Your beauty shines through and makes it all worthwhile.

Discussion Questions

This reader's book club guide is meant to help you examine your own life experience in relationship to the story and themes in this memoir. Rather than focusing just on my life, it is my hope that my story will touch you in a way that inspires you to explore yours.

1. This book describes the arc of Susan's relationship with her sister. Their early childhood was one of a sense of constant companionship, but when they started school, that all changed. How did this new phase of life affect their relationship?

2. What issues does Susan grapple with early in life? How does her relationship to her sister shape her personality and life choices? What does that touch in you about the centrality, or lack thereof, of sibling relationships in your own life?

3. What role does ambivalence play in your relationships with significant others?

4. Susan sometimes fantasized about what Edna would have been like if she were "normal." Have you had fantasies about significant people in your life being different from how they are?

5. The themes of wanting to be normal and feeling like an outsider become more prominent in the story when Susan learns she was born without a uterus and will never bear children. How does that shape the choices she makes in her life? How does this play out in her intimate relationships?

6. Have you ever felt different, or like the odd man out, in your life? Explain.

7. How does being the child of Holocaust survivors weave into the author's themes of being an outsider and being unable to bear a child?

8. Susan came of age in the sixties but grew up in the fifties. How did the span of these decades play a part in her development, as depicted in the book?

9. Within the book, the metaphor of a kaleidoscope is brought in. What is the meaning and significance of it in relationship to Susan's life? How is this metaphor related to the title of the book, *Edna's Gift*?

10. What ways has this book changed or reshaped your awareness of people with disabilities?

11. After reading this book, how do you understand the relationship between brokenness and wholeness? Has your perception shifted?

About the Author

©Chris Loomis

For over forty years, Susan Rudnick, LCSW, has been listening to people tell their stories in her Manhattan practice of psychoanalysis and psychotherapy. In *Edna's Gift* she tells hers. The seed for her memoir was "Coming Home to Wholeness," a chapter she contributed to *Into the Mountain Stream*, a book of personal reflections on psychotherapy and Buddhist experience. Susan, a Zen practitioner, has published haikus as well as articles about psychotherapy in professional journals. Culled from thousands of submissions, one of her haikus appears in *New York City Haiku: From the Readers of The New York Times*. She and her husband live in Westchester, New York, but often love to spend time at their cabin in the Catskills. Being a parent is her greatest joy.

SELECTED TITLES FROM SHE WRITES PRESS

She Writes Press is an independent publishing company founded to serve women writers everywhere. Visit us at www.shewritespress.com.

Change Maker: How My Brother's Death Woke Up My Life by Rebecca Austill-Clausen $16.95, 978-1-63152-130-0
Rebecca Austill-Clausen was workaholic businesswoman with no prior psychic experience when she discovered that she could talk with her dead brother, not to mention multiple other spirits—and a whole new world opened up to her.

Rethinking Possible: A Memoir of Resilience by Rebecca Faye Smith Galli $16.95, 978-1-63152-220-8
After her brother's devastatingly young death tears her world apart, Becky Galli embarks upon a quest to recreate the sense of family she's lost—and learns about healing and the transformational power of love over loss along the way.

Beautiful Affliction: A Memoir by Lene Fogelberg
$16.95, 978-1-63152-985-6
The true story of a young woman's struggle to raise a family while her body slowly deteriorates as the result of an undetected fatal heart disease.

Don't Leave Yet: How My Mother's Alzheimer's Opened My Heart by Constance Hanstedt $16.95, 978-1-63152-952-8
The chronicle of Hanstedt's journey toward independence, self-assurance, and connectedness as she cares for her mother, who is rapidly losing her own identity to the early stage of Alzheimer's.

A Different Kind of Same: A Memoir by Kelley Clink
$16.95, 978-1-63152-999-3
Several years before Kelley Clink's brother hanged himself, she attempted suicide by overdose. In the aftermath of his death, she traces the evolution of both their illnesses, and wonders: If he couldn't make it, what hope is there for her?

All the Ghosts Dance Free: A Memoir by Terry Cameron Baldwin
$16.95, 978-1-63152-822-4
A poetic memoir that explores the legacy of alcoholism and teen suicide in one woman's life—and her efforts to create an authentic existence in the face of that legacy.